THE SHAMBHALA GUIDE TO
KABBALAH AND JEWISH MYSTICISM

The
Shambhala Guide to
Kabbalah
and Jewish
Mysticism

Perle Besserman

Illustrations by *Zoë Trigère Besserman*

SHAMBHALA
Boston & London
1997

SHAMBHALA PUBLICATIONS, INC.
Horticultural Hall
300 Massachusetts Avenue
Boston, Massachusetts 02115
http://www.shambhala.com

9 8 7 6 5 4 3 2 1

FIRST EDITION
Printed in the United States of America

⊗ This edition is printed on acid-free paper that meets the
American National Standards Institute Z39.48 Standard.
Distributed in the United States by Random House, Inc.,
and in Canada by Random House of Canada Ltd

LIBRARY OF CONGRESS CATALOGING-IN-PUBLICATION DATA
Besserman, Perle.
   The Shambhala guide to Kabbalah and Jewish mysticism /
   Perle Besserman.
      p.   cm.
   Includes bibliographic references and index.
   ISBN 1–57062–215–9 (pbk.: alk. paper)
   1. Cabala. 2. Mysticism—Judaism. I. Title.
BM525.B48   1997   97–19190
296.1′6—dc21   CIP

In Memory of Jacob and Lillian Besserman

Contents

Pronunciation Guide

H ERE ARE the meanings and pronunciations of some key words and phrases used in this book, with occasional additional comments.

The pronunciation given corresponds roughly to the Sephardic pronunciation currently used in Israel and, increasingly, in communities worldwide. This is something of a compromise between the Ashkenazic pronunciation of European Jews and their descendants and that of the Jews from Arab countries and theirs.

The sounds used in the phonetic spellings should be pronounced as follows:

a	ago
e	men
ee	seen
o	law
oo	root
kh	loch (Scots), ach (German)
ai	**eye**
ay	**way**

Adam Kadmon, the primordial human being, the cosmic man: a-*dam* kad-*mon*

Adon Olam, Lord of the Universe: a-*don* o-*lam*

Adonai, Lord: a-do-*nai*. Often used as a substitute for YHVH

Assiah, Action: a-see-*ya*

Atzilut, Emanation: a-tzee-*loot*

Ayin, the 16th letter of the Hebrew alphabet: *a*-yeen

Baruch shem kevod malkhuto le-olam va-ed, Blessed be the Name of the glory of His kingdom forever and ever: ba-*rookh* shem k'*vod* mal-khoo-to le-o-*lam* va-*ed*

Bereshit, "In the beginning," the first word of the Book of Genesis: b'ray-*sheet*

Beriah, Creation: b'ree-*a*

Binah, Understanding: bee-*na*

chakikah, engraving: kha-kee-*ka*

chatzivah, hewing: kha-tzee-*va*

Chayyah (sing.), living being; *Chayyot* (pl.): kha-*ya*, kha-*yot*

Chesed, Mercy: *khe*-sed

Chokhmah, Wisdom: khokh-*ma*

Daat, Knowledge: *da*-at.

derash, the allegorical level of interpretation of the Torah: d'*rash*

Echad, One: e-*khad*

Ein Sof, literally, without end; the Infinite No-thingness: ayn *sof*

Eloheinu, Our God: e-lo-*hay*-noo

Elohim: e-lo-*heem*

gematria, number mysticism: ge-*mat*-ree-ya

Gevurah, Judgement: g'voo-*ra*

gilgul, "turning over," reincarnation: geel-*gool*

hitbodedut, "self-isolation," a meditation technique: heet-bo-de-*doot*

hitbonenut, contemplation: heet-bo-ne-*noot*

Hod, Majesty: *hod*

kavvanah (sing.), intention; *kavvanot* (pl.): ka-va-*na*

kelippot (pl.), husks, shells, shards; *klippa* (sing.): k'lee-*pot*, k'lee-*pa*

Keter, Crown: *ke*-ter

maggid, spirit guide: ma-*geed*

Malkhut, Kingdom: mal-*khoot*

nefesh, the vital level of soul: *ne*-fesh

neshamah, the spiritual level of soul: ne-sha-*ma*

Netzach, Splendor: *ne*-tzakh

peshat, the literal level of interpretation of the Torah: p'*shat*

remez, the homiletical level of interpretation of the Torah: *re*-mez

Ribbono shel olam, *Master of the universe*: ree-bo-*no* shel o-*lam*

ruach, the intellectual level of soul: *roo*-akh

Sefer Yetzirah (Book of Formation): *se*-fer ye-tzee-*ra*

sefirah (sing.), sphere, world, emanation, stage of consciousness; *sefirot* (pl.): s'fee-*ra*, s'fee-*rot*

Shaddai: sha-*dai*

shefa, divine "influx": *she*-fa

Shekhinah: sh'khee-*na*

Shema Yisrael, Adonai eloheinu, Adonai echad, Hear O Israel, the Lord our God is One. The quintessential declaration of Jewish faith: Sh'*ma* yees-ra-*el* a-do-*nai* e-lo-*hay*-noo, a-do-*nai* e-*khad*.

Shema, Hear: sh'*ma*

sod, the secret level of interpretation of the Torah: *sod*

Tiferet, Beauty: teef-*e*-ret

tikkun, repairing: tee-*koon*

tzaddik, righteous one: tza-*deek*

Tzevaot, hosts: tz'va-*ot*

tzimtzum, contraction: tzeem-*tzoom*

yechidah, "perfect union," the highest level of soul: ye-khee-*da*

Yesod, Foundation: y'*sod*

Yetzirah, Formation: ye-tzee-*ra*

YHVH, the letters of the Tetragrammaton, or sacred Name of God: *Yod, Heh, Vav, Heh*. This Name is traditionally considered unpronounceable. Jews today commonly substitute "ha-*Shem*," literally "the Name," in everyday speech; "Adonai" in blessings, prayer, or when reading the Torah in a liturgical setting; or, if the letters are referred to specifically, "yod-kay-vav-kay" ("kay" as a substitute for "heh" appears only in this context and is not otherwise part of the Hebrew language). See note 7, page 41, on the Kabbalistic pronunciation of YHVH.

yichud, unification: yee-*khood*

Yisrael, Israel: yees-ra-*el*

The Shambhala Guide to
Kabbalah and Jewish Mysticism

Introduction

What Is Kabbalah?

ACCORDING TO Solomon Ibn Gabirol, the eleventh-century Spanish mystic who named it, *Kabbalah* ("received" tradition) is the "teaching from mouth to ear," a direct transmission of timeless spiritual wisdom. A talmudic adage says that there are as many ways to Truth as there are human faces. Thus the Kabbalah may assume any shape or form. Depending on the "receiver," it may appear as an angel, a holy fool, a Torah scholar, or a beautiful woman. It may be embodied in a book, a song, a dance, or a conversation with God. As with all spiritual traditions, Kabbalah cannot really be taught; it must be experienced. And while its metaphors and history make it a uniquely "Jewish" form of spiritual practice, the kabbalistic experience is universal in that it aims to realize the "No-thingness" of all things.

Emerging from the ancient world of the Middle East and encrusted in exotic symbols, Kabbalah has been regarded as impenetrable at best and dangerous at worst. Like its Christian and Islamic mystical counterparts, its emphasis on individual experience proved threatening to the religious institutional hierarchy, and Kabbalah was forced to go underground. For centuries, the meditation tech-

niques at its core were buried by nervous Kabbalists under an esoteric blanket of terms and codes in the hope of fending off
excommunication from the Jewish authorities and death from the
secular Gentile establishment. Whether it was the Romans in the
first centuries of the common era (CE) or the medieval Inquisition
or the government-organized pogroms of modern Europe that motivated their secrecy, the Kabbalists bore the double burden of being
not only Jews, but Jews who "dabbled in magic." The reputed impen-
etrability of the Kabbalah therefore owes more to social conditions
than to the actual practice itself.

It wasn't until the twentieth century that secular writers such as
Gershom Scholem, Walter Benjamin, Franz Kafka, Martin Buber,
Moshe Idel, and Isaac Bashevis Singer dared to strip the Kabbalah of
its veil of secrecy. Abetted by the demand for opening the teachings
to all, regardless of age, sex, and degree of religious orthodoxy, modern rabbis such as Abraham Isaac Kook, Abraham Heschel, Menachem Mendel Schneerson, Aryeh Kaplan, and Zalman Schachter-
Shalomi responded to the call. Thanks to their translations and the
pioneering efforts of a new generation of Jewish feminists, such as
rabbis Lynn Gottlieb, Susan Schnur, and Shoni Labowitz, the Kabbalah is now accessible to any committed seeker who wishes to practice the "teaching from mouth to ear."

Because it is so intertwined with Jewish history, the best way of
understanding Kabbalah is through its chronology. Its rich store of
imagery is based on the Torah (the Pentateuch, or Five Books of
Moses), the Talmud (rabbinic commentary), and the accumulated
legends of the Jewish people. Although there are no kabbalistic
"schools" as such, the teaching was adapted to the cultural, political,
and geographic needs of its practitioners, and that is why the techniques appear to be so varied. For example, first-century mystics derived their visions of the Throne of God from Ezekiel, chapters 1 and
10, in the Bible; thirteenth-century Kabbalists permuted (arranged
in various combinations) the four Hebrew letters of the Holy Name

of God, YHVH; sixteenth-century communities in the northern Galilee focused on traditional liturgy and prayer; and nineteenth-century East European Hasidim entered meditation through song and dance. The Kabbalah's symbolism was always consistent but never remained static. Jewish spirituality may appear to be wearing a many-colored coat, but there is a basic thread that runs throughout, linking the practices of the ancient rabbis at the Yavneh Academy in Judea in Roman times to those of the California Kabbalist today.

The first organized form of Jewish meditation practice emerged in a sixth-century BCE collection of manuals called *Maaseh Merkavah* (Tales of the Chariot). The goal of those who engaged in it was to achieve direct experience of the Divine by concentrating on a group of mandala-like images that depicted the *hekhalot* (heavenly "palaces") leading to the Throne of God. The illustrious Rabbi Akiva provided a model for all seekers who would travel this path. It is said that he and three of his compatriots "entered the garden," that is, practiced this highly concentrated form of meditation. Unfortunately, the results for all but Rabbi Akiva were less than heartening. One rabbi died of the effort; another went mad; and the third became an apostate. The most important lesson, as all subsequent teachers of the way of the Chariot tell us, is to be like Rabbi Akiva and not make the mistake of separating the life of the Divine from the life of everyday activity. Like all successful meditators, Akiva was able to "come and go"—that is, harmonize spirituality and daily life.

The emphasis on out-of-body experiences distinguishes the visionary practices of the Merkavah mystics from the inner-directed visualizations of the Babylonian school of Hai Gaon (939–1038). Unlike the followers of Rabbi Akiva, whose visualizations sought to induce altered mental states with the intention of experiencing the prototypical visions of Ezekiel, Gaonic mystics focused less on a literal journey through the celestial spheres than on the individual expansion of spiritual consciousness.

Using a detailed cosmological map as a focus for concentration, mystics of the third to eleventh centuries CE practiced a form of meditation described in a manual called *Shiur Komah* (The Body of God). Their Middle Eastern predilection for grand and imaginative storytelling charts the innumerable paths and byways that lead to a discovery of the Divine in God's created worlds. In a group of manuals appearing under the heading *Maaseh Bereshit* (Tales of Creation), the most famous of which is the *Sefer Yetzirah* (Book of Formation), the dynamic, ongoing process combining the "No-thingness" of the Absolute with the ceaseless activity of the relative world is entered through the medium of the twenty-two letters of the Hebrew alphabet and the ten *sefirot*—the worlds-within-worlds that make up the cosmic Tree of Life. To the *Sefer Yetzirah* are attributed the origins of several later branches of the Kabbalah, particularly those using permutations of the Hebrew alphabet and the sefirot as subjects for contemplation.

By fusing permutations of the Hebrew alphabet and the mandala of the ten sefirot, the early Palestinian Kabbalists condensed two meditation techniques into one. In the *Bahir* (Book of "Brightness"), twelfth-century French Kabbalists added to this a variety of meditations on the Tetragrammaton (the four-letter Name of God—YHVH, or the Hebrew letters Yod, Heh, Vav, Heh), including colors and forms, breathing exercises, and bodily gestures—and the "modern" Kabbalah was born.

In 1280, the Spanish Kabbalist Moses de Leon brought the ancient and modern worlds together in the *Zohar* (Book of Radiance), an Aramaic treatise purportedly derived from the mystical writings of the second-century Kabbalist Rabbi Shimon bar Yochai, successor of Rabbi Akiva. The *Zohar* itself was the result of de Leon's mystical experience, emerging from an extended series of meditations on the Divine Name. Couched in a poetic, biblical-sounding narrative, the book is actually a multilayered meditation manual that outlines the higher states of consciousness achieved by those who, with proper guidance from a qualified teacher, "ascended" the sefirotic Tree of Life.

Abraham Abulafia, a rebellious thirteenth-century Spanish Kabbalist, opened the practice to include Jewish women and Gentiles. His prophetic approach to meditation included manipulating the Hebrew letters in a nondenominational context that brought him into conflict with the Jewish establishment and provoked the Inquisition. It was Abulafia's liberal Kabbalah that set the stage for the messianic cults that were to plague Jewish mysticism for the next five centuries, until Hasidism emerged from the ruins in the eighteenth century to revive it. Today's Kabbalist is the direct heir of this mass movement for everyday mystics. Although it is still a highly fractured and disputatious inheritance, Israel Baal Shem Tov's Hasidic version of Kabbalah transformed the complexities of the ancient Chariot meditation—as well as its later offshoots—into a simple "way of the heart." Here, ecstasy takes the place of intellect, joy takes the place of suffering, and devotion takes the place of messianism.

Being closest in time and place to biblical events, the first-century Kabbalists focused on the visionary experiences familiar to them in the Hebrew Bible. With the exile and dispersion of the Jews from the Holy Land, the emphasis correspondingly shifted toward repair of the breach between God and the Jewish people, the people and the land, and the "upper" and "lower" worlds. At the completion of the exile, with the greatest part of the Jewish population living in Europe, Rabbi Akiva's circle was completed by Kabbalists who had so infused their everyday lives with spirituality that the holiest teacher was often indistinguishable from the village fool.

Preparing to Practice

The Torah—a feminine embodiment of God—is the starting point for all Jewish spiritual practice. Kabbalists read "her" on four levels: literal (*peshat*), homiletical (*remez*), allegorical (*derash*), and secret (*sod*). Put together, the first letters of each of these four He-brew words form the acronym *Pardes* ("garden"), which refers to the meditative stages of consciousness achieved through the practice of Kabbalah. As the *Zohar* tells us, this means that, far from being a mere book or even the sacred historical record of God and the Jewish people, the Torah is a living guide to the experience of Truth. All the seeker must do is devote him- or herself to following its instructions. Like Akiva and his contemporaries, those who would seek to en-ter the garden of Truth must make a sincere commitment to Torah practice.

From the earliest days, then, the nature of kabbalistic practice could not be separated from the nature of its practitioners. There are, in fact, almost as many books and pamphlets outlining the prep-arations for meditation as there are guides to the techniques them-selves. One of the most famous of these preparation manuals is *The Book of Directions to the Duties of the Heart*, written by Bachya ben Joseph Ibn Pakuda, an eleventh-century Kabbalist who was also a prominent judge. He divided the self-reckoning process into ten "gates" that led the seeker through the stages prefacing the ideal life of the spirit. Living an ethical life, being pure of heart, and remaining socially integrated continue to remain the touchstones of character for the Kabbalist.

Further refined by Spanish immigrants fleeing to the Holy Land from the Inquisition in the fifteenth and sixteenth centuries, prepa-ration manuals like Ibn Pakuda's were used as practical guides by entire communities. Not unlike the later Quaker "Friends" groups that sprang up in England a century later, the *Chaverim* ("Friends") who flourished in and around the northern Galilee town of Safed held open meetings for meditation and discussion of spiritual and social matters. A model for today's Havurah movement, the Safed Kabbalists, many of whom were sophisticated city intellectuals, re-turned to the simple life of the land, grew their own food, and used Hebrew to conduct their daily affairs. Codes of behavior for the

Chaverim were set by prominent teachers like Moses Cordovero in his *Book of Thirteen Divine Attributes*.

The Kabbalist Community

The mystical community of Safed reached its zenith under the leadership of Isaac Luria (1543–1620), known as the Ari (Lion) because of his high spiritual attainments. At Cordovero's death, the Ari had taken charge of the Chaverim, who now renamed themselves the Lion Cubs. Building on the practices of his Sephardic forbears, but adding the techniques he'd learned as the student of a prominent German Kabbalist in his younger years, Luria devised a set of group meditation exercises based on the standard book of daily prayers used by ordinary Jews. Luria's daily prayer book, however, contained a printed set of *kavvanot*—instructions for breathing and contemplation—to accompany each prayer. Many prayer books today still bear Luria's printed kavvanot, but, since the disappearance of the Safed community of Chaverim, only a handful of their Sephardic Kabbalist descendants know how to decipher and use them.

The Ari introduced another new meditation technique into the daily life of his disciples: the *tikkun* ("repair"), a form of concentration aimed at binding the world of form to the formless Absolute. Assuming responsibility for liberating all of Creation, the Kabbalist meditated no longer as an individual but as a representative of the entire cosmos. For this purpose, Luria gave each of his students a *yichud*, a "unification" exercise, uniquely suited to the individual's temperament and capacity. Coupled with a concentrated mind and body, the Hebrew letters that made up the yichud provided the meditator with a powerful link to the worlds that were revealed by one's expanding consciousness. Accompanying visualizations might include seeing oneself in the form of the great cosmic Tree of Life while breathing rhythmically or performing Sufi-influenced bodily

movements. Far from being an exercise in sensory deprivation, Lurianic Kabbalah utilized every sense in bringing about the unwavering
meditative concentration required by the practitioner of the yichud
method. Even incense, snuff, and fragrant herbs and spices were en-
listed to heighten the meditator's sensory awareness.

The Goal

Regardless of where and when they lived, Kabbalists throughout
the ages have practiced with one goal in mind: being at one with
God. Although some translated this experience in abstract terms,
such as "living in No-thingness," "cleaving to God," or "losing oneself in the Boundless Infinite," all agreed that it could only be accomplished by a human being in this manifest world of created
things. As living, breathing, self-reflective images of God, only
human beings could transport the divine influx into the activities of
daily life—and back again to the Infinite.

1
The Kabbalistic Universe

IT WOULD BE A MISTAKE to regard the Kabbalah's elaborate visions of heavenly palaces and supernatural beings as anything more than symbolic waystations on the path to the One. As the great eighteenth-century Hasidic teacher known as the Maggid of Mezerich warns: "A man should actually detach his ego from his body until he has passed through all the worlds and become one with God, till he disappears entirely out of the bodiless world."[1] This insistence on the absolute No-thingness of the Jewish meditative experience was, and still is, the aim of the true spiritual seeker. Glorious and terrible visions may appear, but they are nothing more than manifestations of the mind and body of the meditator. Personal experience rewarded the ancient teachers with a keen understanding of the human psyche and its trappings. Having confronted their own inner angels and demons and recognized the tragic consequences of an unripe plunge into the depths of the mind, they urged caution even as they gave instruction. Rabbi Akiva exhorted his students not to succumb to hallucinations: "When you enter near the pure stones of marble [a euphemism for a particular stage of contemplation], do

1. From "Collected Sayings of the Maggid of Mezerich," tr. Aryeh Kaplan, in Kaplan's unpublished ms. "Sparks in the Night."

9

not say, 'Water! Water!' for the Psalms tell us, 'He who speaks false-hood will not be established before My Eyes.' "[2]

Since Akiva and his student would be reading the *sod*, or hidden level of the Torah, as a guide for meditation, this scriptural quotation could be regarded as an injunction against taking a mentally created "image" of God for an authentic experience of God. The kabbalistic universe must therefore be understood as a map of the mystic's journey to God, one whose symbols, though grounded in the Torah, have fluctuated with the changing collective Jewish consciousness.

The Map of the Chariot

For his "ascent" in advanced stages of meditation, the early Kabbalist was provided with a readymade vehicle in the prophet Ezekiel's symbolic journey to heaven. Swept into the clouds on a fiery, winged chariot drawn by divine beasts and angelic beings, Ezekiel became the prototype of the ancient Jewish contemplative. The Chariot mystic's journey was so clearly outlined by his biblical predecessor that he knew what to expect even before entering the meditative state. He would pass through seven states of consciousness called the hekhalot before arriving at the Throne of God. There, depending on his degree of meditative absorption, the meditator would encounter the seated form of Adam Kadmon, a cosmic man that represented an archetypal reflection of himself.

To keep from being distracted by the mental projections he might encounter en route, the Chariot mystic used a combination of chants and visualizations. For example, should his path be barred by a demonic guardian, he might picture God's Judgment as a bright red sphere and repeat the Holy Name Adonai until the guardian disappeared. If he were following one of Rabbi Akiva's instruction

2. From "Selections from *Pirkey Hekhalot*," tr. Aryeh Kaplan. Unpublished ms.

manuals, he would have access to a variety of contemplative methods derived from biblical passages and original chants composed by Akiva himself. One of these prepared the meditator for *chaluk*—a vision of light so brilliant it came to be identified with the "robe" in which God was wrapped in order to be perceived by Moses (and, presumably, by anyone else who could attain the contemplative stature of a Moses).

In an exercise called "putting on the Names," the Kabbalist wore a robe inscribed with permutations of the sacred Tetragrammaton, so that, in addition to chanting the names of God, he could physically embody them. There was even an instruction manual for this exercise called *Sefer ha-Malbush* (The Book of Clothing). Bodily signs and postures accompanying different stages of meditation were also available, instructing practitioners on when to stand, sit, or prostrate themselves and how to regulate the breath, and warning them to watch for changes in breathing, excessive sweating, and feelings of faintness or dizziness.

One of the greatest Chariot mystics was Rabbi Nechuniah ben Hakanah. Famous for teaching while actually in a meditative state, he described his experiences to a circle of rapt students while one of his colleagues wrote them down. One imagines that the only thing better than this motivational glimpse into the mysteries of Chariot meditation would be to experience it for oneself.

An influential Kabbalist of the thirteenth-century Provence circle, Isaac the Blind, expanded the symbolism of the Merkavah to encompass all of God's activities in the human realm. His followers used the intricate symbols depicted in the *Bahir* as a symbolic map for discovering traces of transcendent divinity in the manifest world.

FIGURE 1. The Hebrew letters of the Tetragrammaton
(reading right to left): YOD HEH VAV HEH.

The Map of the Body of God

The mystic traveler who reached the Throne and encountered the figure of Adam Kadmon visualized himself journeying through the hairs of the cosmic man's beard. When he lost himself in the divine and glorious light, and was bathed in the holy oil lubricating each strand of hair, the adept was blessed to have attained the spiritual level of Moses. Needless to say, there have been few in this illustrious company: Rabbi Akiva, Rabbi Shimon bar Yochai, Isaac Luria, Abraham Abulafia, and Israel Baal Shem Tov are the only ones who come to mind; and, of course, none but Abulafia would dare proclaim this himself. These "sparks of the soul of Moses" were declared to be such by their worshipful disciples.

The degree of the mystic's meditative attainment was measured according to the development of three levels of the human soul: the vital (*nefesh*); intellectual (*ruach*); and spiritual (*neshamah*). By meditating on the cosmic beard of Adam Kadmon, highly developed practitioners—that is, those with the greatest degree of *neshamah*—could progress quickly in the journey to the One. Once the spiritual portion of the seeker's soul had reestablished its intimacy with its divine source, the anthropomorphic reflection of God in the benevolent form of the Ancient One became his Father, Friend, or Lover—and could be addressed in personal terms. From the Kabbalist's point of view, such soul-binding forms of meditation would account for the very intimate love poetry of the biblical Song of Songs (one of the most popular mystical handbooks), for King David's direct way of addressing God in the Psalms, and later, for the Hasidic Rabbi Nachman of Breslov's "conversations with God."

Meditation on the Shekhinah, the female aspect of God, consisted of visualizing a magnificent woman with seventy faces, each hiding an aspect of the meditator's soul behind a set of elaborate garments. In the most advanced form of soul-binding meditation, the Kabbalist visualized the male and female "bodies" of God in a lovers' embrace.

In doing so, the practitioner correspondingly united the spiritual, intellectual, and instinctual portions of his own soul.

The Map of Sefirot

The cosmic Tree of Life, which contains the fruits of divine emanation, presents us with the most detailed map of the Kabbalist's contemplative journey. Here, the infinite and unknowable God is made accessible to human beings through a descending order of manifest "qualities." Depicted in the shape of a tree whose trunk is divided vertically into "male" (right) and "female" (left) halves, the Tree consists of ten interpenetrating branches bearing sefirot (singular, *sefirah*)—variously translated as spheres, worlds, emanations, or stages of consciousness—each a holographic representation of the

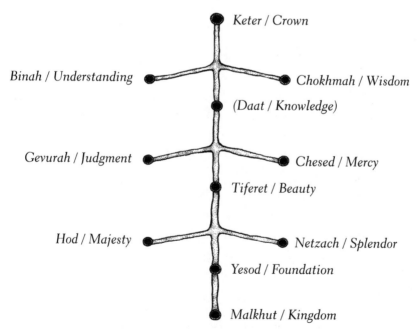

FIGURE 2. The Tree of Life, depicting the ten sefirot plus an eleventh, "hidden" sefirah, Daat.

others. Built on the postulate of "as above, so below," the sefirot embody God's Creation in a Great Chain of Being, reaching from the lowliest inert mineral all the way to the Ein Sof—the Infinite. As Moses de Leon says in the *Zohar*, "God is unified oneness. . . . Down to the last link, everything is linked with everything else; so divine essence is below as well as above, in heaven and on earth. There is nothing else."[3] Thus, by starting from any point on the Tree, the spiritual seeker can locate the way to the source. Yet it is only by *not* constructing images of Ein Sof that one can know it.

All of the apparently differentiated sefirot, then, are actually one with the Infinite and as such cannot be counted or lodged in time. In this nonmanifest aspect, Ein Sof (used here interchangeably with Ein) is beyond sense or imagination and can only be called No-thing. Flowing through the sefirot like clear water, it assumes the variegated colors and forms of the material world. According to Moses Cordovero, "That essence does not change color at all, neither judgment nor compassion, neither right nor left. Yet by emanating through the [sefirot]—the variegated stained glass—judgment or compassion prevails."[4]

The mental journey through the four archetypal, interpenetrating worlds and sefirot of the cosmic Tree requires familiarity with its multileveled symbolism. The map guiding the seeker along its circuitous paths is the *Zohar*, which contains detailed instructions for contemplation of each corresponding divine emanation, human mental function, body part, sacred Name, and color encountered en route. Table 1 (pages 16–18) presents the sefirot, and their locations in the four worlds, listed individually in descending order from the highest, Keter (Crown), to the lowest, Malkhut (Kingdom).

The following sefirot represent the particular qualities associated with biblical figures:

3. Daniel C. Matt, *The Essential Kabbalah* (San Francisco: Harper San Francisco), p. 26.
4. Moses Cordovero, *Pardes Rimonim* (1586), tr. Aryeh Kaplan, unpaginated ms.

Binah	Leah
Chesed	Abraham-Rebekah
Gevurah	Isaac-Sarah
Tiferet	Jacob
Netzach	Moses
Hod	Aaron
Yesod	Joseph
Malkhut	David-Rachel

Most important for purposes of meditation on the sefirot is knowing the correspondences between human stages of consciousness and their divine emanations.

In figure 3 (page 18), an unseen point emanates from Ein Sof, the Infinite void above the Tree. Continuing downward, the energy assumes the shape of a lightning flash and enters Keter. From there to Chokhmah is a point called Yesh (Being). This emanation is called Being from No-thingness and represents the highest point in the world of form. It corresponds to the highest level of human consciousness. A third point, flowing across from Chokhmah on the right side to Binah on the left, completes the divine emanations that make up the highest archetypal world of Atzilut (Emanation). Atzilut encompasses the figure of Adam Kadmon, the cosmic man, and contains the primary forms emitted by the merging of polar energies like the male Chokhmah (Wisdom) and the female Binah (Understanding).

Elaborating on the *Sefer Yetzirah*—whose anonymous authors indicated that there were ten divine emanations but did not assign them names—members of the Gerona school of Isaac the Blind identified the six lower sefirot. They used the qualities of God cited in 1 Chronicles 29:11 as the basis for their choice. Transforming the word *Gedulah* (greatness) to read Chesed (mercy) and *Mamlakhah* (kingship) to Malkhut (kingdom), they assigned each of the six biblical words of praise to a corresponding sefirah. The remaining four

TABLE 1. The Ten Sefirot

KETER / *Crown*

Location on cosmic Tree: Top, Center
Archetypal World: ATZILUT/Emanation
Human Function: Will and Humility
Body Part: Exterior—Top of the Head
            Interior—Brain
Sacred Name: EHEYEH
Color: White/Black

CHOKHMAH / *Wisdom*

Location on cosmic Tree: Right side
Archetypal World: ATZILUT/Emanation
Human Function: Wisdom
Body Part: Right Ear
Sacred Name: YAH
Color: Blue

BINAH / *Understanding*

Location on cosmic Tree: Left side
Archetypal World: ATZILUT/Emanation
Human Function: Understanding
Body Part: Left Ear
Sacred Name: YHVH/ELOHIM
Color: Green

DAAT / *Knowledge*

Location on cosmic Tree: Center
Archetypal World: ATZILUT/Emanation
The hidden sefirah. No manifest correspondences are given, since
    Daat represents direct meditation on Ein Sof, No-thingness.

CHESED / *Mercy*

Location on cosmic Tree: Right side
Archetypal World: BERIAH / Creation
Human Function: Lovingkindness
Body Part: Right Arm

Sacred Name: EL
Color: White

GEVURAH / *Judgment*

Location on cosmic Tree: Left side
Archetypal World: BERIAH /Creation
Human Function: Strength
Body Part: Left Arm
Sacred Name: ELOHIM
Color: Red

TIFERET / *Beauty*

Location on cosmic Tree: Center
Archetypal World: BERIAH/Creation
Human Function: Self-consciousness
Body Part: Heart
Sacred Name: YHVH
Color: White

NETZACH / *Splendor*

Location on cosmic Tree: Right side
Archetypal World: YETZIRAH / Formation
Human Function: Determination
Body Part: Right Leg
Sacred Name: TZEVAOT
Color: Red

HOD / *Majesty*

Location on cosmic Tree: Left side
Archetypal World: YETZIRAH / Formation
Human Function: Flexibility
Body Part: Left Leg
Sacred Name: ELOHIM TZEVAOT
Color: Green

YESOD / *Foundation*

Location on cosmic Tree: Center
Archetypal World: YETZIRAH/Formation

TABLE 1 *(continued)*

Human Function: Spiritual Aspiration
Body Part: Genitals
Sacred Name: SHADDAI
Color: White

MALKHUT / *Kingdom*

Location on cosmic Tree: Center
Archetypal World: ASSIAH/Action
Human Function: Perception
Body Part: Feet
Sacred Name: ADONAI
Color: White

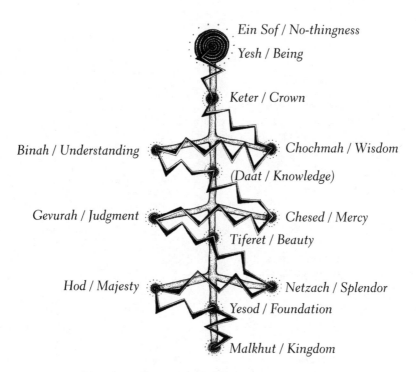

FIGURE 3. The lightning-flash course of emanations from
Ein Sof to the sefirot on the Tree of Life.

qualities—Gevurah, Tiferet, Netzach, and Hod—were left as they appeared in the original biblical version.

The Four Archetypal Worlds

1. ATZILUT emerges from the ten spoken words of God that gave rise to Creation. It contains the first, and highest, manifestation of the ten sefirot, then splits off into four levels, which generate the appearance of the three lower worlds of Beriah, Yetzirah, and Assiah.

2. BERIAH is the manifest world described in Genesis. Corresponding to the seven days of Creation, it containes the seven lower sefirot and is home to the angelic hosts. Guarded by the angel Metatron, Beriah is the bridge between the upper world of emanation and the lower world of formation.

3. YETZIRAH: The tip of the highest point of the archetypal world of Formation rests in the lowest point of the preceding world of Beriah. Its descent into matter therefore makes it less ethereal than the province of the angelic hosts and more accessible to human beings. It corresponds to Eden, the garden of divine and human interaction preceding Adam's descent into the world of Assiah.

4. ASSIAH represents our world of matter, the lower part of which houses the realm of "shells" (kelippot)—unbalanced energies emerging from the shattered vessels, or primordial forms, when God contracted the divine light in order to create the world.

Ascending and Descending

Regardless of whether one chooses to ascend or descend along the branches of the Tree, the aim of the exercise is to dissolve the ego and become one with Ein Sof. Since No-thingness cannot be grasped by the intellect, it must be apprehended in a moment of direct "forgetting" of the self. Someone who wished to begin with Keter, the mediator between the transcendent Ein Sof and the immanent sefirot, would draw upon the humility symbolized by that sefirah, which is required for such selfless action.

Chokhmah, the embodiment of God's "wisdom," represents potentiality in the world of form. Hence, meditation on Chokhmah corresponds to the highest mental activity available to human beings. The energy associated with God's wisdom is masculine, active, and procreative.

Binah, understanding (the receptive, procreative counterpart of wisdom), manifests the Divine in its feminine aspect. Meditation on the link between Chokhmah and Binah brings the fruits of meditation to bear in one's daily life. Harmonizing in oneself the polarities of active wisdom and receptive understanding serves to unite the opposing energies symbolized by the masculine and feminine sefirot on the cosmic Tree.

Chesed and Gevurah emanate directly from Chokhmah and Binah. The masculine Chesed, synonymous with unmitigated expansiveness, represents the infinite power of God's love. Radiating mercy throughout the worlds, this aspect of the Divine is tempered by the feminine power of containment, the power of Gevurah to impose restrictions on the overflow of mercy that might flood the world if allowed to remain unchecked.

Tiferet reconciles the opposing tendencies inherent in Chesed and Gevurah. Metaphorically viewed as the "son" of the two, Tiferet represents the stable center of the cosmic Tree, the personal God of Israel who mediates between heaven and earth. Because this sefirah is most accessible to prayer, it is identified with the liturgy as a daily object of meditation.

Netzach and Hod represent the lower versions of Chesed and Gevurah. They serve as channels for communication of the Divine emanations from above. Corresponding to their status on the Tree, the energy emanating through these sefirot is diluted so as not to overpower its human receivers.

Yesod is the lower transmitter of the energy residing in the secret sefirah, Daat. Reserved for meditation during the Sabbath, when one is believed to be blessed with a second soul (i.e., a greater capacity for concentration on spiritual matters), Yesod represents the opportunity for ascending to the higher levels of consciousness symbolized by the upper sefirot.

Malkhut is the most accessible of God's emanations. Rooted in this world and embodying the feminine aspect of the Divine, the final sefirah represents the sacred nature of the Creation. Meditation on Malkhut is therefore synonymous with "raising the sparks" from the world of matter.

Meditation on colors, sounds, sights, smells, and touch at appointed times, while chanting the appropriate prayers and blessings, turns daily activities such as washing, eating, lovemaking, sleeping, and waking into a life lived entirely through and in God. Constant awareness of one's nonseparateness from the cycles and energies emanating from the sefirot provides a comprehensive method for remaining at one with God at all times.

Using the daily prayer services as occasions for meditation on the sefirot, the Lurianic Kabbalist, for example, would only have to look at the kavvanot accompanying each prayer to know when and how to bow. The writings of Rabbi Chayyim Vital, Isaac Luria's successor and scribe, inform us that bowing unites the head (the uppermost portion of the spine) with the coccyx (the lowermost portion of the spine) and therefore embodies the unification of the upper and lower sefirot. Thus, corresponding to the eighteen vertebrae of the human spine were eighteen blessings to be recited in silence during the Amidah, the "standing" portion of the daily prayer. (The nineteenth blessing that was later added accounts for the coccyx.) Refusing to bow showed a lack of humility and, correspondingly, signaled that one still had the ego of the serpent—which, before it was punished in the Garden of Eden by crawling, had a vertical spine and walked upright. Hence, the biblical serpent in the Garden may be seen kabbalistically as the inability to focus concentration on the highest sefirot. This would be equated with an overriding sense of self that prevents one from bowing.

Since physical, emotional, and spiritual "bodies" were not regarded as separate entities, the sefirot could also be arranged into the primordial human form of Adam Kadmon. Embodying God's reflection, each sefirah on the Tree thus also represents a different "limb" of the divine "body." Ein Sof, God as undifferentiated, pure Being, or No-thingness, remained beyond representation, of course. But with Keter there arose the primordial image of an androgynous human head. Meditation on Chokhmah revealed a bearded male "face" on the right side (representing brain, intellect) and Binah, a corresponding female "face," on the left (representing heart/mind). The right "arm" consisted of Chesed, and the left "arm" of Gevurah. The trunk of the body, particularly the location of the "heart" and spinal column, was identified with Tiferet and was regarded as male. Netzach and Hod were right and left "legs," respectively, and stood for the prophetic realm. Yesod was identified with the genitals and represented both life-energy and the realm of the righteous. Malkhut, the embodiment of Shekhinah, represented the feet, planted in the physical world, and was regarded as female.

The union of Tiferet and Malkhut formed the ground where immanence and transcendence met. In these sefirot lay the secret of returning to the One. This knowledge led the medieval Kabbalist Azriel of Gerona to claim that, insofar as everything exists in Nothingness, all creation is basically undifferentiated.

In their human form, then, the sefirot are the living emblem of coming and going, which brings us back to Rabbi Akiva as one who could come and go—that is, enter the garden (meditate on Nothingness) and leave without harm (apply the fruits of his meditation in the world of form).

After the destruction of the Temple in Jerusalem in 70 CE, the Jewish dispersion introduced a new pessimistic strain into the Kabbalah, one that emphasized exile and separateness rather than union.

The product of the breach between God and the Jewish people was a focus on *tzimtzum*, the "contraction" of Ein Sof or Infinite Absolute, which, by limiting itself to create the world of form, had overflowed into vessels that were unable to contain its power and had cracked them. The kelippot (variously translated as husks, shards, or shells) of the vessels that resulted from this overflow, became our "fallen" world, while most of the divine light returned to the higher sefirot. Nonetheless, some holy sparks remained, and it was the Kabbalist's task to bring these down and repair the vessels—that is, bring the divine light back into the material world. This rather complex form of meditation, known as *tikkun*, or repairing, was central to the practice of the Kabbalists of sixteenth-century Safed. Israel Sarug, a member of that community, described it thus:

> When the shards descended to the bottom of the world of actualization, they were transformed into the four elements—fire, air, water, and earth—from which evolved the stages of mineral, vegetable, animal, and human. When these materialized, some of the sparks remained hidden within the varieties of existence. You should aim to raise those sparks hidden throughout the world, elevating them to holiness by the power of your soul.[5]

The pragmatic eighteenth-century Hasidim turned the tikkun into a less esoteric exercise. They believed that performing any activity, even the most mundane, in a concentrated state of awareness could accomplish the task of "raising the holy sparks." In the early twentieth century, Rabbi Abraham Isaac Kook interpreted "repair" to mean that creation itself is constantly changing, evolving, and ascending, bringing the contemplative to an experience of Ein Sof, which reveals that there is no need for repair and never has been.

Late-twentieth-century Kabbalists have extended tikkun into the

5. Matt, *The Essential Kabbalah*, p. 97.

social and political spheres, particularly as it pertains to healing the breach between racial and ethnic groups, men and women, and industrialized and developing nations.

The Map of Letters

Simplifying the abstruse Hebrew letter meditations in the *Sefer Yetzirah*, the thirteenth-century Kabbalist Abraham Abulafia opened this form of contemplation even to those who knew no Hebrew. Like the twentieth-century Asian teachers who made their ancient Hindu, Buddhist, and Sufi practices accessible to the Western world, Abulafia's travels also took him from his home (Spain) to a distant world (the East) and then back again. A student of Sufism and Yoga and a longtime adept of the Kabbalah, he combined breathing, chanting, body movement, and visualization exercises in a Hebrew prophetic context that still remains unique in the Jewish mystical tradition. Since Abulafia's system was rooted in the *Sefer Yetzirah*, it is impossible to describe his teaching without taking a closer look at his source.

According to the *Sefer Yetzirah*, in addition to embodying God's qualities in the form of emanations, the sefirot also function as the language by which those qualities are conveyed. Complementing visualization on the sefirot, meditation on the Names of God that constitute the very nature of the sefirot focuses less on their denotative meaning than on the pure, nonrational utterances by which they come into being. In other words, the sefirot are both the qualities *and* the language by which the Ein Sof makes itself known. The more adept one is at translating this divine language, the closer one is to the Source. Familiarity with the sacred Names of God is therefore equal to familiarity with God.

Since Keter is beyond form, meditation on the letters of the sacred Names must begin with Chokhmah, container of the inherent, premanifest power of the Divine language. Here, the transcendent Ein Sof is hidden in the as yet unspoken form of the Torah. Chokhmah, therefore, is the repository of the potential forms that would ultimately give rise to the Creation. Inherent in the unwritten Torah, one of the six "things" that existed before God created the world, is the power of the "Wisdom" that gave rise to all Being. Assuming the spiritual forms of the letters as it traveled through the sefirot, this power finally manifested itself in Malkhut, in the physical form of the written Torah. Before emanating downward, the power of Chokhmah assumed four symbolic letters and named itself YHVH. As they journeyed into the other sefirot, the original four letters of the Name designating Wisdom were permuted and combined, appearing as multiple variations of the original. Residing in Chokhmah, the Tetragrammaton (YHVH, God's primordial Name) remained disembodied, identified with the unwritten (male) Torah. Revealing itself through the sefirot, the written (female) Torah, became the manifest body of God in the created world.

According to Abulafia's contemporary, Moses de Leon, author of the *Zohar*, the oral and written Torah are one entity. To the Kabbalist, this means that God's words (that is, the revelation of the unwritten Torah hidden in Chokhmah), resounding at Sinai, were heard as seventy sounds that were simultaneously revealed as seventy lights. This experience of synesthesia (mixing sensory experiences, as in "seeing" sounds and "hearing" lights) was had by all the souls present at Sinai, which included the souls of all past and future Jews as well.

The Kabbalist can have the same experience by meditating on the revelation at Sinai, reliving what his or her soul experienced there. In this context, the letters of the revealed Torah are synonymous with the divine emanations (sefirot)—God's attributes encoded in number, sound, energy, and form. All are one with the letters of the Torah and are therefore interchangeable for purposes of meditation. The attributes, too, are interchangeable, resounding with the hidden Names that God self-assigned. The human body is where the map of sefirot and the map of letters meet.

The seven lower sefirot and their Names correspond to the seven centers of energy along the right side of the spine and represent "male," active energy. "Female," receptive energy resides on the left. Each has its counterpart in the nervous system, which, like the sefirot on the cosmic Tree, meet in Crown, the head, and each has its corresponding set of Names, as set out in the Torah. For example, using the Song of Songs as a form of divine acrostic, the *Zohar* offers symbolic meditations on the energy centers along the spine. Combining meditations from the Chariot, sefirot, and letters, the *Zohar* depicts the halls of the heavenly palace as extensions of the primordial energy point at Crown (Keter) down along the "spine" of the cosmic Tree, encased in its protective neural sheath so that it can withstand the light emanating from above. To experience the light unsheathed, one meditates on the letters of the Torah as the garment of God. (Hence, the robe inscribed with Holy Names that was worn by the Kabbalist is a mirror image of God's own robe of Names.)

The human body, with its corresponding letters and energy centers (sefirot), is intimately connected to the five stages of ascent along the cosmic Tree. Here the soul moves from the animal to the spiritual level, to the level of breath, to the living essence, and finally to unique essence, or oneness. The lowest levels are experienced in sleep as dreams, which represent the animal level's highest function. Meditators will therefore dream of "higher" matters, but their dreams still resonate with the animal elements in their nature. Kabbalists who performed letter permutations had ascended to the breath level; but only those who continued their ascent with no desire for supernatural powers could move through the breath level without doing damage to their minds. (Recall the case of Rabbi Akiva's less fortunate companions.) Divine inspiration could come to the Kabbalist at this phase, but true prophecy, as Abulafia would have it, could only come when the meditator disappeared into the One. The highest, or fifth, level of the soul's ascent was therefore called *yechidah* ("perfect union"). One who attained it was said to be infused with the *shefa* (divine "influx") and was deemed a "prophet." Although infused with the shefa, true prophets like Moses and Akiva remained with God at all times, even when not meditating but engaging in the business of daily life. Such people were always correct in their predictions, for they were intimately linked with Keter, the source of all emanations relating to our world of cause and effect.

On one level below dwelled the spirits and souls of the ancient sages and the Shekhinah Herself, occasionally appearing to the Kabbalist in his letter meditations as the embodied "voice" of the Torah. This fourth level, the stage of breath, was referred to as the place from which the *maggid*, a spirit guide, emerged to help the Kabbalist ascend on the sefirotic Tree of Life.

2
Jewish Meditation

M<small>EDITATING ON THE</small> immanent God manifesting as self (and thereby fulfilling it) is the key to the practice of Kabbalah. Regardless of whether the seeker prefers what Rabbi Aryeh Kaplan called the "structured" or the "unstructured" form, today's Kabbalist has a variety of meditations from which to choose. For the devotional person, there is the Hasidic informal conversation with God. Those preferring a more focused kind of meditation can practice *gerushin*, a form used by the sixteenth-century Kabbalists of Safed that takes a biblical verse as a subject for contemplation. Visually oriented people might prefer concentrating on a candle flame, flower, picture, or place, letting the essence of the object lead them to an experience of Ein, No-thingness. Verbal repetition of prayers, supplications (like Rabbi Nachman of Breslov's *Adon Olam*, "Lord of the Universe!"), or other words or phrases can be used for focusing the mind. Hasidic meditation in particular emphasizes concentrating sensory awareness on sounds, smells, tastes, and body movements (such as dancing or swaying), and focusing attention on daily activities such as washing dishes, cooking, cleaning, gardening, painting, and building. Internalizing the attributes of the sefirot as they appear on the cosmic Tree, more psychological forms of meditation permit one to work with positive emotions such as love and negative feelings such as anger. Nondirected meditation, the most difficult form, goes right to the source by focusing on No-thingness.

The earliest schools of Jewish meditation have been traced back to 400 BCE. Led by the masters we know as prophets, these biblical training centers had more than a million students. As depicted in the Old Testament, their methods adhered to the strict regulations of the Torah and combined chanting, music, and dance. Other forms of meditation, particularly those involving what was considered idolatry, were not permitted.

After the Babylonian exile and the dispersal of these prophetic schools, meditation became the secret province of a few "worthy" initiates. The product of the Book of Ezekiel, Chariot meditation emerged during the period of the rebuilding of the second Temple, further distancing the masses from the complexities of visualization and substituting the eighteen blessings of the Amidah instead. Thus, by the talmudic period (200 to 600 CE), except for exercises in daily prayer, the ancient meditative techniques were too couched in esoteric symbol and allegory to be practiced by most spiritual seekers. Manuals like the *Sefer Yetzirah* and *Hekhalot Rabbati* (Greater Book of Sacred Palaces) were available between 100 and 500 CE, but because they were used by only the most disciplined rabbis of the inner circle, it would take their rediscovery and interpretation by medieval Kabbalists like Abraham Abulafia and Moses de Leon to circulate their techniques on a wider scale. It was left to men like Moses Cordovero and Isaac Luria to further unravel the meditative secrets of Kabbalah for practice by the sixteenth-century Chaverim, and, in the eighteenth century, for the founder of Hasidism, Israel Baal Shem Tov (Master of the Holy Name), to clarify the *Zohar*'s opaque system for the entire Jewish community.

Continuing in the tradition of their founder, the first three generations of Hasidim placed strong emphasis on meditation. But after coming into conflict with the rabbis of the mainstream Jewish establishment, and even being excommunicated for openly practicing Kabbalah, the Hasidim succumbed to the will of the authorities and stopped teaching it. Thus, the entire Jewish meditative tradition was buried once again, not to be resurrected until the twentieth century.

Meditation Techniques

In keeping with the Kabbalah's emphasis on preparation, it is best to introduce its meditative techniques by defining the Hebrew terms in their historical and cultural context. It was Isaac Luria, the Ari, who characterized the state of meditation itself as kavvanah, "concentrated awareness," and hence created the instructive markings called *kavvanot* (plural of *kavvanah*) to accompany the Kabbalist's daily prayers. These instructions for meditation were used in connection with various rituals to "direct the mind along the inner paths defined by the esoteric meaning of the ritual." [1] Deepening stages of concentration included *hitbonenut*, contemplating Creation until one was indistinguishable from it, and *hitbodedut*, exterior and interior seclusion from world and thought. Hitbonenut consisted of gazing at an object without associating anything with it. This non-thinking would bring the Kabbalist to an experience of the interpenetration of absolute and relative worlds. The great twentieth-century teacher Rabbi Abraham Isaac Kook advised his students to "increase aloneness [hitbodedut]" and penetrate the question, "What are we?" in order to "find bliss, transcending all humiliations or anything that happens, by attaining equanimity, by becoming one with everything that happens, by reducing yourself so extremely that you nullify your individual, imaginary form, that you nullify existence in the depth of your self." With the realization that the self is "No-thing," comes "the light of peace. . . . The desire to act and work, the passion

1. Aryeh Kaplan, *Jewish Meditation* (New York: Schocken, 1985), p. 50.

to create and to restore yourself, the yearning for silence and for the inner shout of joy—these all bond together in your spirit, and you become holy."[2]

GAZING

Gazing at one's own hand and repeating the word *Gevurah* (the sefirah of power), or permuting the letters of the Tetragrammaton (Yod, Heh, Vav, Heh)—the Yod to coincide with a coin, the Heh (equal to the number 5) with the five fingers of the hand offering the coin, the Vav with the arm reaching out to give, and the final Heh with the hand of the receiver—condensed three meanings into one: the commandment to give charity, the link between God and human beings, and the attribute of Chesed (the sefirah of mercy). Contemplating five colors in a candle flame (white, green, red, black, and sky blue), with an awareness of their corresponding sefirot, brought one into the presence of the Shekhinah, indicating the attainment of an advanced state of hitbonenut. Continued gazing at any object would produce a *tzelem*, or eidetic image ("aura"), which could also foster the necessary mental quieting for hitbonenut to occur.

In the yichud meditation, the Kabbalist "gazed" at the individual letters of the Holy Name given to him by his teacher, linking them in the visualization with the intention of unifying the male and female aspects of himself as he concentrated on joining the male and female aspects of God and Creation.

Gazing into water, another form of quieting the mind, is a technique found in the Book of Ezekiel. Here the prophet experiences self-realization while gazing into the river Kvar ("Already"), symbolizing the fact that what we are looking for is already right here, always reflected in the "water" of self-consciousness.

2. Daniel Matt, *The Essential Kabbalah*, p. 124.

CHANTING

Hagah, the repetition of words or sounds, was an ancient chanting method for inducing meditative absorption that was reintroduced by David Kimchi, a thirteenth-century Kabbalist, who described it as similar to the "cooing of a dove or the growling of a lion." Repetitive chanting and singing had been the stock-in-trade of meditators in the talmudic period who, in the *Hekhalot Rabbati*, had instructed their students to repeat a specific number of Holy Names 120 times in order to attain the first of the palace halls leading to the heavenly Throne—that is, to deepen their concentration.

Safed Kabbalists selected a biblical verse for this purpose, repeating it over and over until they had penetrated deeply into its intellectual meaning and achieved single-pointedness of mind. Isaac Luria was known for repeating biblical phrases until they embodied themselves as living voices and "spoke" to him This practice of gerushin was further refined by Joseph Caro, a prominent teacher in the Safed community, who repeated portions of the Mishnah (oral Torah) to the point where a maggid "emerged" from the text in the form of a spirit guide to further instruct him.

LISTENING

Listening to sounds with focused attention allows the practitioner to hear the voice of God in everything. The Baal Shem Tov urged his students to direct their awareness equally to prayer, birdsong, rain, or a shout in the street. The Maggid of Mezerich taught that the best way to practice listening was to forget oneself entirely. "You must be nothing but an ear which hears what the universe of the Word is constantly saying within you. The moment you start hearing what you yourself are saying, you must stop."[3] Their Hasidic descen-

---

3. Aryeh Kaplan, "The Light Beyond: Adventures in Hasidic Thought," unpublished ms.

dants continue to remain devoted to listening as a preferred form of meditation, for it can be practiced anywhere and at any time.

Meditation on the Sefirot

As divine attributes linking interlocking worlds, the sefirot represent both preparation and practice. Since the Kabbalist is their living embodiment in this world, it is up to him or her to refine these godly qualities by attending to them at all times. Thus, mentally linking Keter to Chokhmah, for example, is tantamount to infusing one's worldly actions with the spiritual energy emanating from their divine source. To hone the power of concentration and remove the husks of distraction while performing their daily activities, meditators direct their attention to Binah.

Visualizing the cosmic Tree, one takes its right and left branches, respectively, as one's own male and female energies, and harmonizes them by balancing the qualities of Gevurah with Chesed. Neutralizing the power that coincides with Gevurah by meditating on mercy, its counterpart in Chesed, the Kabbalist turns them all to the service of God.

Where the highest sefirah, Keter, is neutral, the descending sefirot are visualized as polarities, assuming the variety of colors, forms, and qualities that correspond to the Kabbalist's field of action. Thus, in situations requiring mercy, one might visualize Chesed, its corresponding color, guardian, mineral, sound, and set of letter permutations. Calling upon Gevurah in those situations requiring strength, one might visualize a red triangle or one of the guardians connected with that particular sefirah while reciting the appropriate series of sacred Names according to a technique called swallowing: to the visualized sefirah the Kabbalist adds the appropriate angelic name, which is pronounced while holding the breath and moving only the larynx and tongue. The meditation would be a short one, bringing an instantaneous result. As one's ability increases, these brief moments of meditation grow more compact, bringing the Kabbalist to the point of losing all self-consciousness. At this stage, it could be said that the meditator has merged with the sefirot themselves.

Each sefirah is associated with its own time of day, so meditation on the sefirah Malkhut, ruler of night, for example, should be practiced just before going to bed. Since midnight meditation is the province of the Shekhinah, the Kabbalist would visualize Malkhut in her guise of "Beloved." At dawn, before morning, afternoon, and evening prayers, which are ruled by Chesed, Gevurah, and Tiferet, respectively, the meditator would concentrate on the patriarchs corresponding to the sefirot, visualizing Abraham as Chesed, Isaac as Gevurah, and Jacob as Tiferet. This conscious identification with the patriarchs turns one's daily cycle into a comprehensive method for concentrating the mind and living perpetually within the highest sefirot on the cosmic Tree.

Since Chokhmah and Binah are respectively represented by a circle and a square, one could gaze at these geometric forms as they occur in nature at any time that one wishes to sanctify an action. Since action is movement in space and time, the Kabbalist was enjoined by Moses de Leon in the *Zohar* to emulate Abraham, the prototype for all those seeking to achieve oneness with God. Thus, like Abraham, the personification of Chesed, the Kabbalist would have to "descend into Egypt," the world of desire, before attaining his or her objective. Avoiding the example of Noah—who became drunk on the "wine" of desire and could not complete the journey— the practitioner of sefirah meditation would have to remain firmly concentrated on Chesed regardless of what he or she might encounter on the way. Following in Abraham's footsteps, the meditator would enter the Holy Land and "build an altar"—that is, pass through each sefirah en route, emptying oneself in order to make a clear space for mercy to enter. Using the breath to help empty the mind of distracting thoughts, the Kabbalist is advised to breathe as evenly and rhythmically as the sea. Likewise, emulating Isaac meant enduring the supreme test of self-sacrifice personified by Gevurah, while emulating Jacob, the prudent patriarch, entailed pursuing Tiferet by losing oneself in the beloved (Malkhut, Rachel).

Letter Meditation

According to Genesis, the word is the power by which God creates the world. Hence, since the three primordial letters of Creation (Alef/Air; Mem/Water; Shin/Fire) contain the elements connected with the breath, and thus with the generative power of the Word, in both their potential and manifest forms, they channel the energy sustaining the universe. And because human beings, too, are made up of these elements, meditating on the primordial letters is a means of uniting with the entire Creation. In this context, letters are used not as language, for purposes of communication, but as vehicles for the experience of pure being.

The Hebrew alphabet provided Kabbalists with a convenient package that condenses name, form, number, and dimension. Combined with visualization of the sefirot, permutation of the letters of the Tetragrammaton could bring one to a direct and powerful experience of No-thingness.

Meditation on the letters of the sacred Name corresponding to the sefirot on the cosmic Tree begins with Keter. Reciting *Eheyeh*, the sacred Name found at the level of Keter, brings one to the formless world of No-thing, the Source from which all created things emerge. *Yah*, the first expression of the sacred Names in Chokhmah, is made up of Yod and Heh, the first two letters of the Tetragrammaton. The uppermost point of the letter Yod (') represents the first emanation of the sacred qualities of Ein Sof transmuted through Keter. Reciting the name Yah while visualizing Chokhmah and its attendant symbols brings one to a level of consciousness equivalent to the emanation of divine Wisdom in Yetzirah, the archetypal world of formation. Reciting the Name Elohim while visualizing the sefirah

Binah and its attendant symbolic forms brings one to the level of divine Understanding embodied in Heh, the second letter of the Tetragrammaton. The Vav, whose numerical equivalent is 6, represents the course of divine emanations, and their equivalent meditative states, through the six lower sefirot (states of consciousness) from Chokhmah to Yesod. The final Heh of the Tetragrammaton completes the process by materializing the emanations from Chokhmah to Yesod through the physical vehicle of the Kabbalist's body and mind. The sefirot containing these attributes were still regarded as human conceptualizations, however, which had to be broken through as the mind ascended to the realm of pure being without thought. This was most often accomplished by reading a biblical phrase until it made no sense, repeating the now "meaningless" phrase in combination with controlled breathing exercises and bodily movements, and contemplating the letters of the phrase as they "rearranged" themselves.

The authors of the *Sefer Yetzirah* divided letter meditation into a series of stages or gates, each divided into paths that were further subdivided into parts. The first two gates of entry were called the Gate of Heaven and the Gate of Saints (Inner Gate). One began the journey through the gates by visualizing oneself as an angel. Chariot guardians, such as Ariel, Rafael, and Gabriel, as well as others listed in the rabbinic writings, were emblematic of the various psychophysiological states that accompany meditation. Mentally reformulating these angels into the letters that make up their names, the adept could change negative states into positive ones. Terrifying images that might hamper the voyager's progress could therefore be reduced to meaningless phrases. Like meditation on the halls of the heavenly palaces and the cosmic Tree of Life, letter permutation could also bring about hallucinations and fearsome visions. The practitioner was therefore enjoined to subdue such unsettling manifestations by personifying them as letters and reassembling them to form godly thoughts and phrases. Like Rabbi Akiva before him, Abraham Abu-lafia also warned his students about what to expect:

> After much movement and concentration on the letters the hair on your head will stand on end . . . your blood will begin to vibrate . . . and all your body will begin to tremble, and a shuddering will fall on all your limbs, and . . . you will feel an additional spirit within yourself . . . strengthening you, passing through your entire body . . . [like] fragrant oil, anointing you from head to foot.[4]

The *Sefer Yetzirah* points out that not only did each letter of the Hebrew alphabet equal a number, but that these numbers could be used to permute the letters of the Tetragrammaton to induce mystic states of consciousness. (See table 2.) The fact that each letter of

TABLE 2. Hebrew Letters with Their Numerical Equivalents and Tetragrammaton and Sefirotic Correspondences

א	Alef = 1	י	Yod = 10	ק	Kof = 100
ב	Bet = 2	כ	Kaf = 20	ר	Resh = 200
ג	Gimel = 3	ל	Lamed = 30	ש	Shin = 300
ד	Dalet = 4	מ	Mem = 40	ת	Tav = 400
ה	Heh = 5	נ	Nun = 50	ך	Final Kaf = 500
ו	Vav = 6	ס	Samech = 60	ם	Final Mem = 600
ז	Zayin = 7	ע	Ein = 70	ן	Final Nun = 700
ח	Chet = 8	פ	Peh = 80	ף	Final Peh = 800
ט	Tet = 9	צ	Tzade = 90	ץ	Final Tzade = 900

First letter, Yod, of YHVH = Chokhmah
Second letter, Heh, of YHVH = Binah
Third letter, Vav, of YHVH = Tiferet
Fourth letter, Heh, of YHVH = Malkhut

4. Abraham Abulafia, *Sefer ha-Tzeruf*, tr. Aryeh Kaplan, Bibliothèque Nationale ms. no. 774 and Jewish Theological Seminary ms. no. 1887.

the Tetragrammaton represented a sefirah gave Abulafia the idea of blending sefirah visualization and *gematria,* or number mysticism (that is, inner- and outer-directed meditation techniques) to produce a condition of prophetic ecstasy.

"Passing through the gates" was a symbolic way of describing gematria, the increasingly complicated form of letter permutation that accompanied each stage of the contemplative journey. Using gematria, the Kabbalist not only grafted new words and phrases onto the early ones but began calculating numerical values, spelling out their names and the names of the new numbers emerging from the permutations, reversing the alphabet, and reconstructing the letters themselves. On moving from the first to the second gate, the adept calculated and reversed the letters of the Tetragrammaton "inscribed" on one's own body and mind. The practice of *chakikah* ("engraving") involved the ability to visualize the letters of the Tetragrammaton, Yod-Heh-Vav-Heh, and their permutations with unwavering intensity. Isolating each letter from all other mental images was called *chatzivah* (hewing). Instructions on engraving and hewing appear in a manual written by the medieval Kabbalist Shem Tov Ibn Shem Tov, who advocates holding the breath and visualizing the letters the way God did in contracting the divine light and leaving the world in darkness. This meditation technique is aligned with Chokhmah, one of the highest sefirot in the archetypal world of Atzilut, which is located beyond the realm of thought. The Kabbalist would have to hew a path beyond conceptualization in order to *become* Chokhmah. In other words, meditating on the letters of the sacred Name Yod-Heh-Vav-Heh leads to unification with the godly attributes represented by the sefirot.

In the act of meditation (hitbodedut), aloneness and at-oneness—differentiated and undifferentiated worlds—become synonymous. The illustrious medieval Kabbalist Isaac of Akko thus instructs the student to "place in front of the eyes of your mind the letters of God's name, as if they were written in a book in Hebrew script. Visualize every letter extending to infinity . . . when you visualize the letters, focus on them with your mind's eye as you contemplate infinity. Both together: gazing and meditating."[5]

The letter permutations following the condition of seclusion (another word for meditation) would begin with *mivta*, "articulation" of the letters constituting the Name or phrase or verse with which one had chosen to work. Next would come *mikhtav*, actually "writing" them down, and finally, *mashav*, "contemplating" them. *Dilug* ("skipping") was the process of observing the mind as it free-associated from one idea to another according to a set of flexible code words, and substituting one letter for another. Thoughts and images were thereby turned into sentences, further broken down into words and letters, and then into pure, wordless energy, or shefa.

Progressing from this visionary stage, the Kabbalist moved beyond permuting individual words, phrases, and letters to combining letters and their numerical values. After calculating ordinary words, one would begin calculating the numerical value of the sacred Names, reversing them, contemplating their inherent attributes, and permuting them according to a variety of vowel combinations. Looking at the letters inscribed in the Torah as if they were a black flame upon a white background induced a condition in which the entire Scripture could be permuted into an acrostic of seventy-two sacred letters emerging from the original Yod-Heh-Vav-Heh. Dropping self-consciousness altogether resulted in obliterating all distinctions and *becoming* the Torah herself. Here are Abulafia's instructions for entering the meditative state by permuting the four letters of the sacred Name:

> Take each letter of the Name and vocalize it with a long breath. Do not breathe between two letters, only hold the breath for as long as you can, and then rest for one breath.

5. Matt, *The Essential Kabbalah*, p. 120.

Do this with each and every letter. There must be two breaths with each letter, one to hold it in during the utterance which *moves* the letter, and one for rest in the interval between every letter. . . . Each single breath is [comprises] an inhalation and exhalation. Do not pronounce the word with the lips between the exhalation and inhalation, but allow the breath and vocalization to emerge while you are exhaling. Visualize the nostrils and mouth in the form of the *segol* ∵ [vowel point for the sound *eh*]. You must know the letters by heart to perform this exercise.[6]

The student would move the sounds throughout the energy centers of the body that corresponded to each letter and its permutations. Charting the breath and combining each letter of the Name with another letter selected from the Hebrew alphabet, one would begin with the Yod (the primal point of the manifesting Ein), consecutively bringing it downward through the four archetypal worlds and sefirot represented by each corresponding letter of the sacred Names. Accompanying visualizations of the head as the element of fire, the heart as air, and the belly as water completed the descent of the energy from the highest world of spirit to this world of matter.

Isaac of Akko developed a form of letter meditation based on Moses' Sinai encounter with Ein. Visualizing images of air, mountain, and fire, the adept "climbed" to the highest level of contemplation, lifting his eyes to gaze into the empty sky until images of sky and earth met to produce a void. Visualizing a circle in that void, and "inscribing" in it an acrostic abbreviation of the entire Torah, the adept gazed at each tightly crammed letter, seeing it as if it were stamped on white parchment. Under the Kabbalist's gaze, the parchment would turn to white fire and the letters to winged forms of deepest black. Gradually, the entire vision would spin to form an

6. Quoted in Perle Epstein, *Kabbalah: The Way of the Jewish Mystic*, p. 96.

undifferentiated blur, bringing the adept to the stage beyond thought to No-thingness.

A technique described in the *Zohar* combines the air, fire, and water that make up the breath in conjunction with permuting the letters of selected words in Ecclesiastes. Arranging the letters for "vanity" (*hevel*) to read "my breath" (*hevli*), which, combined with the altered breathing patterns that resulted from visualizing a column of air rising from the base of the spine to the white matter of the brain, would lead one directly to "no-thought" and prepare one for the experience of No-thingness.

Holidays such as Sukkot, the Feast of Tabernacles, provided symbols for visualization exercises, too. For example, visualizing the spine as Malkhut, in the form of a palm branch, and chanting *Adonai*, then visualizing the heart as Tiferet, in the form of a citron, and chanting *YHVH*,[7] was one way of binding heaven and earth.

Meditation on incense (which was placed on an altar in the Temple) became an aid to reducing anger. All one had to do was concentrate on the calming scent and also visualize the smoke as the rage coming from the instinctual portion of the soul. As the letters constituting the "smoke" dissolved, so did the anger, unifying spirit and matter in the process, and transmuting the quality of fire from destructive to life-giving.

---

7. Before the fall of the Temple in Jerusalem in the eighth century CE, the sacred Tetragrammaton was deemed "unpronounceable" by anyone but the High Priest. The tradition of chanting the sacred Name was maintained by the Merkavah mystics of the Tannaitic period that followed, and continues as an essential part of Jewish mystical practice today. Kabbalists chant the Name in their meditations, combining its individual letter pronunciations with specific breathing exercises that are believed to have been derived from the original teachings of the prophets. The first letter of the Name—Yod (Y)—is pronounced "Yah," the exhalation of the breath coinciding with the long "ah." The second letter—Heh (H)—is silent, part of the exhaled "Yah" sound. The third letter—Vav (V)—is pronounced "Veh," the exhalation coinciding with the "eh" sound. The final letter—Heh (H)—is silent, part of the exhaled "Veh" sound.

The Kabbalist might choose to rebuild the Temple, using his or her own body as a component in the building process. Here, the engraving and hewing of letters substitutes for the physical activities involved in building. Constructing the edifice of letters, one would come upon a series of "quarries" corresponding to the four archetypal worlds in descending order: first, the Quarry of Souls (Atzilut); second, the Quarry of Angels (Beriah); third, the Quarry of Darkening Light (Yetzirah); and finally, the Quarry of Husks (Assiah). Binding each letter to its corresponding attribute, the adept would have to have perfect concentration in order to penetrate the myriad "membranes" that separate the worlds.

Using the Shema, the daily recitation of God's Oneness with all things—"Hear O Israel, YHVH is our God, YHVH is One"—the authors of the *Sefer Yetzirah* reversed the three primordial letters (Alef, Mem, Shin) in a brief but powerful meditation exercise. Breathing the sounds of the letters while pronouncing them, one is instructed to visualize their individual meanings in ascending order as: Shin/fire, chaos; Mem/water, harmony; and Alef/the silence of No-thing-ness.

SHIN   MEM   ALEF

Binding the letters in a yichud, the Kabbalist reenacts the original process of creation. "Since the world was created with Ten Sayings ["And God said . . ." appears ten times in Genesis 1], and the sayings consist of Letters, the Letters are seen as the primary ingredients of creation. Thus, when one contemplates the Tetragrammaton, the Letters serve as the means through which a person connects himself to God and the creative process."[8]

8. Kaplan, *Jewish Meditation*, pp. 74–75.

Even the ascent to Ein and the experience of the No-thingness of the self can be accomplished through intensive concentration on rearranging the letters of the word No-thingness. (When rearranged, the word for "self," *Ani* [Alef, Nun, Yod], becomes No-thingness, Ein [Alef, Yod, Nun].) The four stages of this form of meditation, known as Jacob's Ladder, are action, speech, thought, and no-thought. These correspond to the four letters of the Tetragrammaton:

> *Yod* = action = hand/body
> *Heh* = speech = breath
> *Vav* = thought = spirit
> *Heh* = no-thought = experience of No-thingness

Kabbalists use the four divisions of their morning prayers to correspond to the four stages of meditation on Ein. These consist of an introductory set of readings, verses of praise, the recitation of the Shema and its blessings, and the Amidah. References to the animal sacrifice represent sacrificing the "animal" nature in oneself and becoming a fit spiritual vessel for the divine influx. Focusing on the word *Yisrael* (Israel) as *yashar-El* ("straight" or "right," hence close to God), the Kabbalist recites the Shema—commanding oneself to "hear" as one proclaims Adonai to be one (*echad*) with Creation. In Hebrew, the gematria of the word *echad* (Alef, Chet, Dalet) is 13 $(1+8+4)$, the same as for the word for love, *ahavah* (Alef, Heh, Bet, Heh, or $1+5+2+5$). By thus losing oneself totally in meditation on the Shema, the Kabbalist effects a yichud, binding the sefirot of Malkhut and Chesed in love.

Where the emphasis in the Shema is mental, the Amidah meditation is more physical. It consists in closing the eyes and silently reciting the 42-word blessing of the first paragraph that carries the practitioner through the four stages. Symbolically harmonizing body, mind, and spirit, the Amidah meditation is performed with the feet together, in a standing posture facing in the direction of Jerusalem (in North America, one would thus face east). Bowing with bent knees at each recitation of the word *blessed*, found at the beginning and end of the first paragraph, the practitioner bows from the waist on addressing God (*You*, the second word) and again repeats the bow at the beginning and end of the penultimate section of the Amidah. The prophet Ezra, primary author of this first-century "group meditation," instructs the practitioner to bow down quickly but rise slowly, head first, uncoiling the spine like a snake. Kabbalists of the talmudic period were said to meditate for an hour on the Amidah, reciting one word every seven seconds. Rather than searching for meaning or really "reciting" in the true sense of the word, devotees of the Amidah continue to use the words as a way of losing themselves in Ein.

Bringing the spiritual into everyday life is called *yerudat ha-shefa*—the culminating, fifth stage of meditation that transforms even the most mundane act into a celebration of oneness. Yoked with the upper sefirot, the Kabbalist's daily affairs now serve as a bridge unifying God and Creation. With the Torah as a living guide, the practitioner becomes a physical, mental, and spiritual vehicle, infusing the world with the divine energy of the sacred Names. For the Torah and her commandments are the Vav—the extended hand representing the sefirah of divine mercy, Chesed, the living evidence of God's presence in the physical world. Uniting the Vav and final Heh of the sacred Name each time a commandment is performed with concentrated awareness, or kavvanah, is the equivalent of drawing the divine influx into ourselves and our world, making of our own bodies a dwelling place for Shekhinah. As the thirteenth-century Spanish Kabbalist Joseph Gikatilia taught: "God . . . created in the human body various organs and limbs—hidden and revealed—as symbols of the divine structure. If one succeeds in purifying a particular organ or limb, it becomes a throne for the sublime, inner reality, called by that name: 'eye,' 'hand,' or any other one."[9] Meditation on

9. Matt, *The Essential Kabbalah*, p. 82

any limb—that is, performing any of the 613 commandments in the Torah, no matter how mundane—allows us to perceive the formless workings of the Divine in the world of form.

Prayer as Meditation

The intimate relationship between God and the devotional spiritual seeker is the basis for all meditative prayer. The Baal Shem Tov advised:

> With every word and expression that leaves your lips, have in mind to bring about a unification. Every single letter contains universes, souls and godliness, and as they ascend, one is bound to the other and they become unified. The letters then become unified and attached to form a word. They are then actually united with the Divine Essence, and in all these aspects, your soul is included with them.[10]

There are limits to the mind, places where reason cannot go. It is here that the seeker must continue on, carried along by faith. If, like one of the four rabbis who "entered the garden," we attempt to grasp the experience of No-thingness with thought, we lose our minds. If we go there arrogantly, filled with a sense of our own importance, we destroy ourselves and everything we touch. Hence it is no surprise that humility accompanies will in the Crown, the highest sefirah on the cosmic Tree, and that devotion is the way to get there.

Under Rabbi Akiva's guidance, the Merkavah mystics used the "ascent" through the heavenly palaces as mental excursions offering a "glimpse of the Beloved." But even this intimate experience of oneness had to be sacrificed if one wished to move beyond ecstasy to No-thingness. Yet, more than any other commandment, it was

10. Baal Shem Tov, quoted in Aryeh Kaplan, "Sparks in the Night," unpublished ms.

love of God that compelled the seeker onward. In the tribal world of the ancient Middle East, an entire set of family-oriented symbols appeared to contain the strong cultural emphasis on kinship. The "small" face of Adam Kadmon (the Cosmic Man envisioned on the Throne), for example, corresponded to the familiar, loving Father, the God referred to intimately as You, and even as the meditator's Beloved. The Ancient One associated with the left side of the "face" was linked to Gevurah, representing God as the strict administrator of Judgment. The Ancient of Days, known as "Father of all Fathers," found his complement in the merciful "right" side of the face.

Depending on the seeker's preference, the immanent God could be visualized as either male or female, father or mother, lover or friend. From these relationships emerged the symbolism of the Divine Marriage and the Mystic Bride and Bridegroom that later appeared in the writings of Christian mystics. Such meditations allowed feelings to flow freely as the meditator, with eyes closed, was immersed in a world blazing with color and dancing with light. Ascending the cosmic tree or rising through the halls of the heavenly palaces, one might "hear" the letters and "see" the sounds emanating from the sefirot, each reflecting its corresponding metal, planet, angel, and human body part. If absorption deepened, the meditator might see the lights begin to shift positions, one mounting to the left, another descending to the right, and still another entering between them. One student of Lurianic Kabbalah recorded an experience in which two sefirot crowned themselves with a third, three merged into one, and one suddenly emanated a burst of color. Six sefirot descended all at once, doubled to twelve, became twenty-two, diminished to six, and increased to ten. Finally, the entire kaleidoscope was swallowed up in one great light.

Coinciding with the sefirah Tiferet, this colorful portrayal of the ecstatic condition of the seeker on "meeting the Beloved" is said to take place when one contemplates the Song of Songs. Encountering God as power or Judgment, the seeker would use the language and imagery of awe associated with Ecclesiastes and Gevurah. Wishing to enlist God as righteousness, one would meditate on the passage from Proverbs 10:25, "The righteous one is the foundation of the world," and visualize Yesod, the cosmic pillar of the world—along with its attendant color, element, and sacred Name.

Hasidism represents meditative prayer in its most highly developed form. Less structured than its talmudic, Zoharic, Abulafian, or Lurianic models, it nonetheless encompasses them all. It was Israel Baal Shem Tov's genius for simplifying the complexities of ascending, binding, and permuting, for example, that managed to turn even the least learned of his disciples into expert meditators. All they had to do was bind themselves to God all day and all night through their prayers. Prayerful living provided an ongoing opportunity for unity, bringing each individual into a state of oneness while simultaneously uniting God and Creation. From the Hasidic perspective, then, the experience of Ein is occurring moment by moment and therefore requires no seclusion. Radically redefining the meaning of hitbodedut, the Baal Shem Tov taught that God, meditation, and daily activity were one and the same and that kavvanah, concentrated awareness, was not to be reserved only for sacred occasions but had to be practiced at every moment. The degree of devotional intensity thus became the yardstick of the Hasid's ability to bring holiness into the world. Meditation was employed as part of daily life to glean the divine sparks from any and all activities. With the intention of uniting all the worlds to their Creator, the Hasid visualized himself as a pillar channeling the divine energy throughout Creation.

With prayer serving to balance one's excursions between Ein and daily activity, the Baal Shem Tov's disciples went right to the divine essence of the letters in beginning their recitations. Those who were inclined might practice more complex forms of meditative prayer, combining yichud, visualization, and letter permutation with breathing and chanting, but most Hasidim weren't even bound only to the formal liturgy of the printed prayer book; any words would do.

The Baal Shem Tov taught that every physical thing, including the Torah and prayers, was composed of the twenty-two Hebrew letters and that everything was assembled in a form that, as contemporary Kabbalists have discovered, resembles the DNA base in combination. Made of the same "stuff" as the sefirot, advanced meditators could therefore lose themselves in No-thingness by merely standing in daily prayer, their chanting or spontaneous singing seen as direct expressions of their Creator. Those less advanced were advised to close their eyes while at prayer and to visualize the letters of the words they were reciting. Levels of absorption were symbolized by the three archetypal worlds that were revealed during meditation:

"Nearness" in the archetypal world of Assiah (Action) on the sefirotic Tree meant that self-consciousness was still present.

"Nearness" in the archeytpal world of Yetzirah (Formation) was finer, but still included dualistic images from *outside*.

"Nearness" in the archetypal world of Beriah (Creation) meant that dissolution of the self in No-thingness had been accomplished.

Wrapped in tefillin (phylacteries), the Hasid knew that his forehead box stood for Chokhmah and his leather arm straps stood for Gevurah. Working on quelling distracting thoughts, he divided all thought into seven modes, equal to the seven lower sefirot, noting each thought as it occurred and "placing" each on its appropriate branch. Negative thoughts thus bound to the Tree were neutralized by the Hasid's love and awe. Another means for dealing with disruptive thoughts was to dissect them letter by letter and permute the letters so as to transform "bad" thoughts into "good" ones. (For example, permuting the word *Ani*, I, into *Ein*, No-thing, served to move the meditator away from self-consciousness toward oneness with God.)

In preparing for occasions of formal meditative prayer, the Hasid would first immerse himself in the *mikvah*, or ritual bath. Since the Torah prohibits wearing linen and wool together (Deuteronomy 22:11), he would avoid wearing clothing made of wool when he put on his linen prayer shawl. Lastly, he tied a cloth belt around his waist to demarcate the "upper" and "lower" worlds. In the tradition of his kabbalistic forbears, he might take a pinch of snuff or light a stick of incense. Then, prostrating himself and lifting his hands toward heaven, he put his face between his knees and touched his forehead to the ground. If advised by his teacher to stand while meditating, he might either sway a little or, depending on his teacher's instructions, he might refrain entirely from moving.

The Baal Shem Tov's successor, the Maggid of Mezerich, placed strong emphasis on the realization of No-thingness. To that end, his own successor, Shneur Zalman, developed the *niggun,* a form of meditation using wordless melodies to evoke the "colors" associated with the sefirot Chesed (white), Gevurah (red), and Tiferet (white). On hearing his teacher begin the niggun and taking up the song, the Hasid entered the first three stages of absorption: (1) outpouring of the soul, (2) spiritual awakening, and (3), self-forgetting. Aaron of Karlin, another of the Maggid's disciples, accompanied Shneur Zalman's niggun with dancing.

Rabbi Nachman of Breslov, the Baal Shem Tov's great-grandson, took the founder's informal approach a step further, instructing his Hasidim to use idiomatic terms in the Yiddish vernacular when practicing the spontaneous meditations he called "conversations" with God. Nachman rejected all intellectual or speculative methods, preferring to catch God's attention with the "tears," "screams," and "foolishness" of a child. He deviated from the teachings of his great-grandfather by advocating concentration on this very moment only and rejecting the founder's emphasis on watching and transmuting distracting thoughts during meditation.

Nachman's version of hitbodedut was unique, and he is still regarded as eccentric by the majority of Hasidim. Believed by some contemporary scholars to have suffered from depression, Nachman set aside daily periods for a form of meditation called "heartbreak." His instructions show that, despite the modern scholarly diagnosis,

Nachman clearly understood the difference between depression and the longing for union with God, for he enjoined his students to turn all their longings and sorrows, pack all their personal problems and fears, into the yearning to reunite with the "Father of all Fathers." In his meditation of the heart, Nachman instructed the Hasid to concentrate on this longing for unity (*devekut*) with the Almighty by meditating on the heart of the cosmic body, visualizing himself as a "limb" of God. When the meditator had experienced an unusual surge of ecstasy, he would know that he had found the "limb" from which his own soul had come. From that point on, a Hasid would think of that particular portion of the prayer as his very own.

Another Breslover meditation technique, like the Zen koan, instructs the practitioner to concentrate on an existential question throughout the day and night. Among those that Nachman assigned to his students were "What will become of you?" "What will you do in the end?" and "What will you answer to the One who sent you?"

However, it was not the eccentric Nachman but the Maggid's more intellectual successors who prevailed. Beginning with Shneur Zalman, what had once been a spontaneous and devotional practice was turned into a highly philosophical enterprise. Zalman emphasized locating Daat, the "secret" sefirah on the cosmic Tree, hidden between Chokhmah and Binah. This, he believed, was where the mind connected to the idea of God before transmitting it to the emotional centers. Wisdom represented the initial flash of divine consciousness, and Understanding was the reflection of that flash on the physical plane. Assigning his technique the acronymic name Chabad (Chokhmah, Binah, Daat), Shneur Zalman bypassed the seven lower sefirot and instructed his students to meditate on the ineffable upper three, Chokhmah, Binah, and Daat. Focusing on the intricacies of the *Zohar* and neglecting the Abulafian forms of letter meditation under Dov Baer of Lubavitch, Zalman's son and successor, the Chabad followers formed the nucleus of today's Lubavitcher Hasidic movement. Dov Baer taught his students to narrow their field of visualization and locate the sparks of their own souls as they issued from a great flame, then to gaze at this spark until all sense of its separateness disappeared. Meditation on Ein resulted in *hitlahavut*, absorption in the Absolute, which was characterized as "tearing the illusory veil" that separates oneself from God.

Advanced forms of meditation included instructions for more elaborate visualizations on the upper three sefirot, along with their accompanying breathing exercises. But the Lubavitcher's emphasis was always on No-thingness, on merging the physical and formless worlds by eliminating the ego. To this end, working to refine one's instinctual nature required strict concentration on the performance of good deeds and awareness of the Absolute in prayer. The commandments provided the Chabad Hasid an opportunity for becoming perfectly egoless while performing daily activities, and studying the Torah became a device for uniting human Understanding and divine Wisdom, with thought—the ethereal "food"of the soul—functioning as mediator between the two. Prayer was the occasion for the Hasid to link oneself to the Creator. But, unlike the Breslover's emotional "conversations" with God, it consisted of mostly silent concentration on liberating oneself from the illusion of separateness. Physical acts were thus spiritualized, particularly those involving benevolence toward others.

Dov Baer continued his father's tradition of enumerating five physical and five spiritual paths, portrayed as "ladders" for meditation. This was criticized by rival Hasidim like Aaron of Staroselye, who claimed that it intellectualized meditation to the point of excluding the heart altogether. Aaron argued that most Hasidim could not relate to No-thingness without Chesed, and that the Lubavitcher model was too cold and dry, not devotional enough for a community bound to God by its enthusiasm. Dov Baer responded that he had seen ecstasy, or the search for ecstatic states, result in emotional problems when practitioners did not achieve their goal of uniting with God. Because of that, he recommended the sudden, spontaneous "lightning flash" experience of the Divine instead. Calling it "the simple sound which proceeds from the breath of the heart,"[11] he insisted that merely listening to, for example, the single blast of the ram's horn without entertaining any images was the best way to unity. Dov Baer's radical monism was implemented in two forms of meditation: Looking, simply studying things as they are, without any imagery or thought; and Probing, following a thought to its source in the realm of "nonthinking." At their deepest level of absorption, these meditations would reveal that "the variety of existence is only an 'appearance' and that ultimate reality is undivided and One."[12]

11. Kaplan, "Sparks in the Night."
12. Kaplan, "Sparks in the Night."

3
The Teacher-Disciple Relationship

The Israelite Nation

THE ZOHAR LIKENS THE teacher-disciple relationship to that which exists between the human soul and the Shekhinah. This kabbalistic reading of a talmudic simile refers to the *chavraya*, "mystical companions," who are called the face of the Shekhinah "because [the] Shekhinah is hidden within them. She is concealed and they are revealed."[1] Since the Shekhinah dwells where there are no distinctions, we must take this to mean that, at its deepest level, the entire spiritual community is none other than the Shekhinah herself. In the condition of pure being, there are no mystical companions, no spiritual seekers, for there is nothing to seek. There is only the play of energy that manifests divine immanence. But the act of "ascending" and "descending" throughout the worlds is dynamic, and the Holy Mother assumes many guises. One of the most important of these is the "Community of Israel," and, for Kabbalists in particular, the mystical companions within that larger community who devote their lives to bringing her into their midst. As Judaism is communitarian to begin with, and Kabbalah by its very definition

---

1. *Zohar,* quoted in Matt, *The Essential Kabbalah,* p. 210.

involves a group rather than an individual practice, there can be no discussion of individual roles without first considering the greater role of the community itself.

The formation of the entity called the "Israelite nation" traces back to the revelation at Sinai, which appeared not to one person, but to a community of more than 600,000 souls. Although the Jews' history of sporadic settlement and lengthy dispersion would seem to militate against the forging of a strong national identity, the mass spiritual illumination occurring at Sinai was apparently powerful enough to inscribe the descendants of those souls for the next three thousand or so years. The written Torah and the code of laws emerging from that original experience served to implement the Sinai revelation, affecting the daily life of the Jewish community from the biblical era to the present. But even from its inception, individual members of that community have struggled to keep the original Sinai experience from becoming a metaphor. Because they insisted that the Torah was a continuing spiritual revelation open to experience by all, such voices were marginalized. Whether glorified as prophets, righteous holy men, and sages, or spurned as heretics and madmen, those who sought a direct experience of God were forced into isolation, left with no choice but to create a mystical community within the greater Jewish community.

The Jewish mystics had assumed the double task of becoming one with Torah as well as living according to its codes and commandments. It was this emphasis on the direct experience of living in, and as physical manifestations of, God that alienated them from the mainstream and eventually pushed them to practice in secret. Anyone who would dare read and try to apply the "hidden" Torah was (and in many quarters still is) suspect to many rabbis who resented the notion that such esoteric knowledge was open to interpretation by the masses. Warned by the mystics themselves of the dangers, one can imagine what it would be like to embark on such an enterprise even within the safe confines of a mystical camaraderie, much less attempting it alone. For the practice of Kabbalah demands a lifelong commitment to remaining grounded in the daily commandments while simultaneously climbing the spiritual ladder to God with each mundane task. This means being so absorbed in a state of kavvanah, so bound to God as to be indistinguishable from God. Seen this way, the Kabbalist literally embodies the commandment to love and cleave to God for as long as one lives.

Living so intimately with the Torah can be a tricky business. Therefore even those who would interpret Scripture in a mystical context had to base their interpretations on experience, anchor it in tradition. How could one otherwise tell a genuine experience from a false one? The fact is, one couldn't. Seekers simply had to follow their instincts, letting their faith and Jewish pragmatism guide them. The best yardstick was an empirical one. To paraphrase Maimonides: A prophet is "legitimate" if what he or she says comes true. In other words, one simply had to experience the teaching for oneself. Here is sixteenth-century Kabbalist Moses Cordovero's advice on the subject:

> Try to learn from someone who has followed paths of integrity as far as possible, for the treasures of God have been entrusted in that person's hands. Do not chase after those that boast of their knowledge. Their voices roar like the waves of the sea, but they have only a few spoonfuls of wisdom. Many times I have experienced this myself.
>
> This has also befallen some authors, who compose books with riddles, rhyme, and flowery language; their words are encumbered by excess. . . . The books to which you should cleave, in order to improve, are the compositions of Rabbi Shimon bar Yochai, namely the various parts of the *Zohar*. Of the books of his predecessors: *Sefer Yetzirah* and *Bahir*. Of more recent works: *The Fountain of Wisdom*, [Tales] *of the Chariot*, [Tales] *of Creation*, and similar writings.
>
> Peruse these books in two ways. First, go over the language

of the text many times, taking notes to remember fluently. Do not delve deeply at first. Second, study with great concentration, according to your ability. Even if it seems that you do not understand, do not stop, because God will faithfully help you discover hidden wisdom. As a parent trains a child, so does God purify one engaged in this wisdom, little by little. I have experienced this innumerable times.

If something in this wisdom seems doubtful to you, wait. As time passes, it will be revealed to you. The essential reward of this wisdom is derived from waiting for the secrets that will be revealed to you in the course of time. . . .

Those who persevere in this wisdom find that when they ponder these teachings many times, knowledge grows within them—an increase of essence [insight]. The search always leads to something new.[2]

Unfortunately, even the most well-intentioned spiritual seekers made mistakes. The most famous of these occurred a century after Cordovero, when Smyrna-born Sabbatai Zevi, a self-proclaimed "messiah," led thousands of his cult followers into penury, apostasy, and death. The few Kabbalists remaining after the debacle continued practicing in secret, until Israel Baal Shem Tov brought the teachings to light again in the eighteenth century. Like the circle of Cubs that formed around Isaac Luria in sixteenth-century Safed, the Baal Shem Tov's original Hasidic disciples dispersed after the death of their teacher. What followed was almost a replay of the Sabbatai Zevi story: Hasidic cults springing up everywhere around "masters" who proclaimed all other "masters" but themselves to be false. During the nineteenth century, the biblical idea of the *tzaddik* ("righteous" person) was, in some circles, misinterpreted to represent a messianic figure rather than an inspirational teacher. With the Euro-

2. Matt, *The Essential Kabbalah*, pp. 160–163.

pean Hasidic communities increasing so exponentially as to almost fragment themselves out of existence, the meaning of mystical companionship thus became the source of much bitter sectarian squabbling. It was left to the Holocaust to finish the argument. If many rabbis themselves saw Kabbalah as a dangerous hidden project, what was there to prevent the powerful anti-Semitic governments of Europe from using the notion of a "secret" Jewish conspiracy as an excuse to eliminate the Jews?

Mystical Companions

Taking refuge from its enemies inside and outside the Jewish establishment, the Kabbalah became a strictly personal matter, passed, quite literally, "from mouth to ear." In other words, the teaching was transmitted orally from teacher to disciple, both to ensure its integrity and to protect it from the uninitiated. Consequently, two themes run consistently throughout the writings of the Kabbalists: (1) discovering the practice and locating mystical companions is up to the individual, and (2) the degree of commitment determines the results. Although it differs from the scholarly understanding of Torah that preoccupies many mainstream rabbis, Kabbalah remains an experiential practice that requires no less discipline. The irony is that there is nothing really "hidden" about it. As Menachem Mendel of Peremishlany, an eighteenth-century Hasid, observed: "Whoever wants to learn—the book is readily available. . . . Rather, the secrets hidden throughout the *Zohar* and the writings of the Ari are based entirely on cleaving to God [through meditation] . . . for one worthy to cleave."[3]

What are the characteristics that make one "worthy"of membership in the mystical community? Because it subsumes them all, righ-

---

3. Matt, *The Essential Kabbalah*, p.162.

teousness would be foremost. Since Kabbalists know that they are cast in the image of God, they must strive to become truly righteous, that is, a living condensation of God's commandments. The more egoless one becomes, the more Divinity shines through one. The higher one climbs on the sefirotic Tree (emptying oneself of ego), the easier it becomes to dissolve in Ein, No-thingness. According to Martin Buber, such a person is filled with the primeval light of God. This sanctifies not only the Kabbalist's deeds, but the words of those that relate them. "The miracle that is told," says Buber, ". . . acquires new force; power that once was active, is propagated by the living word and continues to be active—even after generations."[4]

Attention would be the first step on the path to righteousness, for conducting an intensive study of Creation elevates the seeker to a state of awe in the face of God's power, represented by Gevurah. Being brought to Understanding (Binah) by this study of the created world, the aspirant learns to serve God without desire for reward. At this stage, prayer is less a vehicle for obtaining heavenly favors than an occasion for union with the Beloved. No longer performing the commandments out of obedience or fear of punishment, the seeker is said to have reached the stage of humility, the Crown on the cosmic Tree. Thus the righteous are also called the proven, "those who stood the test," and their disciples are called Hasidim, the "pious." (Paradoxically, of course, one can never claim to have "reached" anything, for the practice consists of continual ascending and descending, a commitment to the ongoing refinement of character and bonding with God.)

Because every spiritual trait must be concretized in the physical world, even the most advanced of the righteous must collapse the boundaries between the sacred and the ordinary by living the commandments. This can be accomplished only by one steeped in the

---

4. Martin Buber, *Tales of the Hasidim: Early Masters*, p. v.

practice of meditation under the guidance of just such a teacher. Martin Buber describes: "He can teach you to conduct your affairs so that your soul remains free, and he can teach you to strengthen your soul, to keep you steadfast beneath the blows of destiny. . . . He does not relieve you of doing what you have grown strong enough to do for yourself. He does not lighten your soul of the struggle it must wage in order to accomplish its particular task in this world."[5] This relationship between teacher and disciple binds the community of mystical companions, creating a spiritual force-field that radiates throughout all Creation.

The Tannaitic Sages

Although there is considerable evidence of the existence of "prophetic schools" numbering as many as a million students during the late biblical period, the best-known prototype for all kabbalistic communities is the group of Merkavah mystics such as Rabbi Akiva, in the first two centuries CE, known as the tannaitic period. Devoted to practicing mentally and physically exhausting visualization exercises, the sages in Akiva's circle took safety in number. Basing their "excursions" on the instructions found in meditation manuals such as the biblical Book of Ezekiel, *The Lesser and Greater Hekhalot, Merkavah Rabbah, Shiur Komah,* and *The Book of Enoch,* members of the group helped each other along during the course of their meditations. This created a public forum of sorts within the mystical community centered at Yavneh, with more experienced practitioners guiding initiates through the complexities of the Merkavah, or Chariot mysticism.

A variety of teachings emerged from the original circle, each bearing the stamp of a particular personality. The greatest of these, Rabbi Akiva, around whom the most illustrious sages gathered, can be seen

5. Buber, *Tales of the Hasidim: Early Masters,* p. 5.

as the father of postbiblical Jewish mysticism. He and his loyal disciples were all put to death at the hands of the Romans, leaving only the legendary Rabbi Shimon bar Yochai and his son, Eleazar, to carry on the tradition while hiding from the Romans in a cave. Emerging after thirteen years and learning that there was no longer anyone interested in his teaching, Rabbi Shimon returned to his cave to meditate for another year. The result of this period was a further determination to spread the teachings of the Merkavah, and Shimon once again returned to society. Gradually, a group of committed spiritual seekers gathered around him, and the next generation of mystical companions was born.

As documented in the *Zohar* in the thirteenth century, and continuing to form the mainstay of Kabbalism to this day, the crux of Rabbi Shimon's teaching is that there are no distinctions between our world and the "higher" worlds, that "all souls form but one unity with the Divine Soul." The purpose of our life as humans is to experience this as the underlying fact of existence, and in doing so, to simultaneously unify all Creation with its source, for God simultaneously represents the source and purpose of Creation, the formed and the formless worlds.

Since its written and oral form were one in expressing God's immanence, the Torah was the perfect vehicle for producing such an experience. Embodying the seventy lights and sounds that formed the basis of all Creation, the Torah had revealed herself in the mystery of Sinai; and, manifesting as Malkhut, she continues to reveal her divine attributes in the sefirot. For purposes of meditation, there are no distinctions between the letters of the Torah, the sacred Names, and the worlds-within-worlds on the cosmic Tree. Meditation on these reveals that the practitioner oneself is a living, breathing combination of divine Names, sounds, and letters.

Rabbi Shimon instructed his students to spend part of each day concretizing this fact in meditation. To begin with, he urged them to unify the male and female aspects within themselves by visualizing the ascent of left and right spinal sefirot to the neural realm of "nonthought" in the white matter of the brain. Once they had harmonized their own polar energies, they could advance to meditation on the higher sefirot by visualizing the attributes illuminating their bodies and minds as letters, each with its corresponding color, sound, element, spirit guide, and body part. To accompany the exercise, he recommended that they recite a verse from Song of Songs (4:8) reminding them of the corresponding body parts they would be contemplating:

> Come with me from Lebanon [brain], bride, with me
> from Lebanon! Look from the top of Amana [throat],
> from the top of Senir and Hermon [tongue],
> from the lion's dens [teeth], from the mountains of leopards [lips
> and speech].

All this was to be accomplished by controlling and directing the course of the breath, using techniques resembling those of pranayama yoga. In reciting the Shema, for example, Rabbi Shimon taught students to focus on the three names contained in the blessing (Adonai, Eloheinu, and Echad) as the fire, air, and water that make up their own breath, while visualizing their corresponding sefirot, Keter, Chokhmah, and Binah.

Like his Merkavah forebears, Rabbi Shimon's meditations were rooted in biblical symbolism. Claiming Gevurah as his own particular domain, he designated it as synonymous with Ecclesiastes. For those mystical companions who aspired to Tiferet, he recommended focusing on Song of Songs; and to those drawn to Chesed, he advocated meditating on Proverbs. Analogies from nature abound in his teachings, particularly those having to do with the geometrical forms of things. These include the interlocking triangles of the Star (or Shield) of David, used as a mandala for visualizing the four archetypal worlds; the circle denoting the sefirah Chokhmah; the point of the letter Yod, symbolizing the first manifestation of Ein in Keter; and the square representing Binah. Although they may be difficult for the uninitiated to penetrate, Rabbi Shimon's mandalas provide clear-cut instructions for anyone who is willing to practice Torah. Since every word of the Torah is the living essence of divine wisdom, and every biblical story represents a phase of the meditative journey to oneness with the divine No-thing, *practicing* Torah is more important than merely studying it.

In addition to Rabbi Shimon, those in Akiva's Merkavah lineage who left written records include teachers such as his successor, Rabbi Ishmael, and eleventh-century rabbis such as Chananel ben Chushiel, Nathan ben Yechiel, and Hai Gaon. Rabbi Ishmael presented his disciples with instructions that included chanting and visualizations and were designed to bring them into the company of Merkavah ancestors like Shimon ben Gamliel, Eleazar the Great, Eleazar ben Dama, Yonatan ben Uziel, Yehudah ben Bava, and Akiva himself. Featuring Nechuniah ben Hakanah (one of the most revered practitioners of Chariot meditation), a typical set of Rabbi Ishmael's instructions describes a gathering of mystical companions, both living and dead, preparing for the journey to the Throne:

> . . . all the masses of companions stood on their feet, for they saw streams of fire and flames of light separating between us and them. And Rabbi Nechuniah ben Hakanah sat and arranged before them all the words of the Merkavah, its descent and ascent, how one who descends shall do so and how to ascend. When one wishes to descend he would call to Surah, "the prince of the face," binding him with an oath one hundred-twenty times, using the Name Totrosyai . . .[6]

Medieval Mystics

Rabbi Nechuniah's visionary style of Chariot meditation continued to be practiced long after his death, but only in secret, for by the

6. Quoted in Epstein, *Kabbalah: The Way of the Jewish Mystic*, p. 41.

end of the Common Era, very few of the original mystical companions were left to pass it on. It wasn't until the twelfth century that his instructions surfaced again—this time far from the Holy Land, in Provence, France—in a manual called the *Bahir*. Scholars are doubtful that the work was actually written by Rabbi Nechuniah, but regardless of who wrote it, the familiar visualization guidelines are there, leading seekers who gathered to meditate in mystical companionship through the stages of awe, love, and yearning that would bring them to the Throne of God.

Appearing in the thirteenth century in Spain, the *Zohar*, which purported to be a newly discovered record of Shimon bar Yochai's life and teachings, is now generally thought to be the work of its supposed editor, Moses de Leon. A gifted Kabbalist in his own right, de Leon probably felt he would lend authenticity to the medieval school of Merkavah mysticism to which he belonged by appending to his book the name of one its most revered ancient teachers. Moreover, as a Kabbalist practicing in Spain during the height of the Inquisition, disseminating the teaching by pretending to have rediscovered a "classic" text was probably as much a defensive tactic as it was bold. As noted above, spiritual knowledge is experiential, not intellectual, and the two cannot be judged by the same standards. From the Kabbalist's standpoint, it would therefore be inaccurate to refer to a meditation handbook like the *Zohar* as a "forgery," as some recent scholars have done. Judging from the book's contents (meditation exercises disguised as an anthology containing the tales and sayings of Rabbi Shimon and his band of mystical companions, love poems celebrating the Shekhinah, prayers, and mystically interpreted biblical stories), de Leon was fairly accurate in transmitting the Merkavah of his illustrious ancestor. In addition to keeping the practice safe from the Inquisition, the *Zohar*'s opacity kept it from being misinterpreted by de Leon's potential rabbinic opponents. While any of his kabbalistic contemporaries would be able to understand the book, the nonmystics in the Jewish establishment surely would not.

Moses de Leon's Spanish contemporary, Abraham Abulafia, had no such compunctions. This "people's prophet" opened the fellowship of mystical companions to anyone who refuted the intellectual approach to Torah and sought enlightenment by contemplating her letters. Continuing in the tradition of the Merkavah mystics, Abulafia demanded that his students undergo the same ritual purification, fasting, and self-discipline prescribed by his ancestors. But unlike them, he was unwilling to wait for the approval of his community before disseminating the teachings. Emerging as a self-proclaimed "prophet" while still in his early thirties, Abulafia gathered disciples from all walks of life, Jewish women and Gentiles as well as Jewish men who up until then had formed the core of mystical companionship. In addition to being a charismatic teacher, Abulafia was a prolific writer who left many meditation manuals, including an autobiography, *Hidden Treasure Garden*, that outlined the course of his life and teachings.

In 1280, the year the *Zohar* appeared, Abulafia openly denounced Pope Nicholas III for his anti-Semitism, was tossed into prison in Rome, and, precisely in accord with his own public predictions, was freed twenty-eight days after the pope's sudden death. Surrounded by loyal disciples wherever he went, Abulafia then fled the wrath of the rabbis, moving to Messina, Sicily, where he remained for a year. In 1290, he made another controversial public pronouncement—this time claiming that the messiah would make his appearance that very year—which brought the rabbis down on him once again and forced him to move on to Malta.

The Abulafian Kabbalists maintained intimate ties with their leader. To deem students worthy and assure a harmonious atmosphere among them, Abulafia personally administered tests to all who applied to work with him. These were designed to discern the seeker's character and commitment and to test the applicant's ability to permute the Hebrew letters. If the first test resulted in failure, the applicant was given another chance—this time without being aware of being tested. If at this point the applicant failed, but then returned after revising the error, he or she was taken back. Abulafia was apparently a lenient master, for he offered the faltering student three more chances after that, installing the person in a "probation" period, during which no meditation exercises were given. Resisting any of the tests resulted in the student's dismissal. Those who passed were inducted in a ceremony that included both Abulafia's verbal commitment to the student and the presentation of ten written permutations on the secondary Names of God.

Once proven, disciples were directed away from images and conceptual thought in their exercises, for Abulafia believed that only meditation on No-thingness would usher in the Messianic Age. To that end, he turned from the elaborate visualizations of the Merkavah mystics to simply gazing at the letters of the sacred Name, YHVH, constructed in the form of a chariot. Elucidating the teachings more openly than his contemporary, Moses de Leon, Abulafia taught that the lights and sounds appearing in meditation were actually neurophysiological events, manifestating stages of transformation in consciousness. All one had to do to enter the realm of "no-thought" was to glance at the letters of the Torah without searching for their meaning. He therefore instructed students to stop "reading" the Torah and merely let her reveal herself as the combination of sacred Names that formed her substructure. With this came the warning against attempting to use these techniques for magical purposes.

Another circle of Kabbalists practicing *tzeruf* (letter permutation) formed around Abulafia's contemporary, Isaac of Akko. In a book called *Otzer Chayyim* (Treasure of Life) Isaac attempted to prove that permuting letters was the quickest, surest path to the experience of God. Unlike Abulafia's community, however, the mystical companions at Akko were ascetics who devoted themselves to meeting the arduous demands of their leader. Where Abulafia granted applicants several opportunities to prove themselves, Isaac offered only three, judging their degree of renunciation, devotion, and prophetic ability in a much shorter time period. Isaac's unremitting emphasis on achieving No-thingness, without bothering to linger on the "lower" stages, resulted in a corresponding demand for extreme detachment. This ascetic style of practice was called *histapkut* (frugality, contentment). Though the tzeruf techniques were basically the same as Abulafia's, Isaac made a few additions of his own to highlight the "sin" and "suffering" aspects of the practice. For example, students at Akko were encouraged to repeat the mystical martyrdom of Rabbi Akiva and his companions in their meditation, and to commemorate it by denying themselves sensual pleasures.

Nonetheless, Isaac and his mystical companions at Akko were the exception to the rule, for most Sephardic Kabbalists focused on God as Beloved, seeking union instead of martyrdom. Their medieval German counterparts, however, brought martyrdom to a level surpassing even that of the dour Isaac. Choosing to envision God as Judge, the Ashkenazi (Germanic) Kabbalists gave a new and decidedly ascetic twist to the meaning of awe as it was outlined by the early Merkavah mystics. Calling themselves Hasidim ("pious ones"), German Kabbalists demonstrated their yearning for oneness by rolling naked in the snow, immersing themselves in icy water in winter, and, in summer, smearing their naked bodies with honey in order to attract stinging bees. Although their name is the same as the later movement that couldn't be more different in its approach, the German Hasidim of the Middle Ages left no record of their teachings beyond the observations of their bewildered contemporaries.

The Mystics of Safed

It wasn't until the fifteenth and sixteenth centuries in Safed that mystical companionship achieved a status rivaling that of the tannaitic sages. Indeed, disciples of the most illustrious master of the period, Isaac Luria, believed that their teacher had been reincarnated from a "spark" of Rabbi Akiva's soul, and they themselves from the souls of Akiva's original companions. Because it took root in the Holy Land and had the same climate and geography as a backdrop, Luria's community could easily model itself along the lines of its ancient forbears. Nonetheless, several great Kabbalists had preceded Luria, the Ari, in seeding the mystical ground of Safed. Joseph Caro, who had been "ordered" there by his spirit guide, had arrived in 1536 to head a group that included Moses Cordovero. Cordovero's brother-in-law, Solomon Alkabez, founder of the Chaverim, was already a famous Kabbalist in his own right. Under his leadership, the group meditated at the graves of the ancient companions so as to link up with them and turn their own hearts and minds into abodes of the Shekhinah. Alkabez enjoined his students to speak among themselves in Hebrew, particularly on the Sabbath, and to call attention to each other's ethical lapses.

Another Kabbalist, Rabbi Isaiah Horowitz, was at the center of a Mishnaic Brotherhood whose members learned to recite the Mishnah (oral Torah believed to come from Sinai, compiled by Rabbi Judah ha-Nasi—"the Prince"—around 200 CE) from memory in order to induce mediumistic trances that would bring them into the company of departed spirits. Selecting chapters of the Mishnah and beginning with the consonants that spelled out the name of a departed relative, the practitioner would chant the resulting mantra until he felt he had eased the dead person's spirit. Joseph Caro, Horowitz's contemporary, and the author of the *Shulchan Arukh*, or Code of Jewish Law, which guides the life of religious Jews to this day—added meditation on the Shema and its accompanying breathing exercises to the procedure. Eventually, a maggid, or spirit guide, appeared from the Mishnah in the form of Shekhinah to guide Caro through the exercise. Mediumship was not uncommon in Safed, nor were angelic appearances. Luria's maggid, for example, used to appear while he was meditating in order to lead him to the "heavenly academy" of his choice. Depending on his mood, the Ari could choose to study with the departed spirits of Rabbi Akiva, Nechuniah ben Hakanah, or Shimon bar Yochai. All he had to do was direct his concentrated mind to the "soul root" of the departed master.

Still, it was only after he had purified himself according to the rules outlined in Moses Cordovero's manual on ethics, *The Thirteen Divine Attributes*, that the Safed mystic would be ready to practice such advanced forms of meditation. The basic preparation exercise consisted of visualizing one's body as the Tree of Life and focusing on a desired trait or sefirah. If, for example, the meditator wished to cultivate humility, he would concentrate on Keter in association with his own head. This would remind him not to walk with his head held high, avoiding the eyes of his fellows. Next, he would focus on his brain, always reminding himself to keep his thoughts on God. Concentrating on his forehead would remind him to keep a cheerful open face to the world; visualizing his ears brought undistracted listening to the word of God reverberating in the sounds of daily life; and so on. In private interviews with his students, Cordovero was thus able to judge the degree and intensity of their kavvanah. Having proved himself to the master, the aspirant was then given a more advanced yichud to use in uniting all the worlds on the sefirotic Tree whenever he meditated.

Bearing the secrets of the *Zohar*, Isaac Luria arrived from Egypt in 1570 to initiate a new course for the Safed mystics. With the help of Syrian-born Chayyim Vital as his earnest scribe and primary disciple, the Ari introduced the method he called tikkun to accompany yichud, which was already being practiced by the Chaverim. To purify the student embarking on the tikkun (which was designed not only to repair the "fallen worlds" but also to end the Jewish exile), he assigned him a personal yichud combining a particular sefirah with its appropriate color, sound, angelic guardian, and letter permutation. Perhaps it was because he was so ethereal, living and teaching from the highest levels of the cosmic Tree, that Luria's instructions required translation by the more earthy Chayyim Vital. The first disciple's secret record of the teachings was reverential, filled with stories of miracles performed by the master. Circulated against his wishes after his death, Vital's record brought the complexities of the Lurianic Kabbalah to the level of the ordinary devotee beyond the Safed circle. Here, for example, is a typical purification exercise that the Ari might have designed for one of his Cubs who was preparing to perform a yichud.

1. Make an anonymous donation to charity before entering the synagogue.
2. Bind yourself in your phylacteries and wear them throughout the entire morning prayer service.
3. Take stock of your behavior in the last twenty-four hours. Have you scrupulously avoided harming any living thing? This includes killing insects on your person. If so instructed, have you avoided using a knife when eating? Have you refrained from eating salt? Kept your feet aligned while making the blessings? Kept from distractedly plucking at your beard? Recited the appropriate chant given you when putting on your clothes?
4. Choose the best day and time among those allotted to you for performing spiritual duties.
5. Repeat the phrase "I am God who heals you" (Exodus 15:26) in combination with your own set of permutations on the letters of the Tetragrammaton (YHVH).[7]

To avert the outside forces of distraction and help focus attention, the Ari might have provided the student with a formula. Perhaps he told him to meditate on the top of his head in absolute silence, visualizing the point of No-thingness emanating into the Crown sefirah. Walking outdoors, he could imagine his legs as the sefirot of

7. Epstein, *Kabbalah*, pp. 22–23.

Netzach and Hod, Splendor and Majesty. Regardless of the exercise, everything depended on the intensity of his concentration, for it was this that would serve to unify the Name of God with its source in the Crown sefirah.

Properly prepared for the yichud, the advanced disciple could begin to redeem the world as he bound himself to his maker in meditation. The Ari might remind him that the colors he would see in the sefirot were not really physical colors but attributes, or energies flowing through them. He would thus recognize that his own imagination was creating form and color to contain God's Wisdom, Understanding, Judgment, and the like. Unshaken by the sights and sounds encountered on his ascent, the Lurianic Kabbalist could then calmly embark on the reversal required by the tikkun, perhaps the most difficult part of his meditative journey. Drawing the light from the highest sefirah attained on the ascent, he would begin the descent. This time, however, he would be using the divine influx gathered in his own body and mind to infuse every creature in every world along the way. In this fashion, even the lowliest beings in the lowest worlds on the cosmic Tree were elevated and united with their Source.

Despite their identification with the ancient mystical companions, Luria did not believe his Cubs to be up to the task of enduring the hallucinations experienced by Rabbi Akiva and his circle. To keep them from harm, he had them concentrate only on those sefirot that had shaped their particular souls. A highly developed practitioner might be able to bind his soul with that of a great departed sage in order to get help for the journey (hence the practice of lying prone on the graves of illustrious Kabbalists in order to absorb the energy of a shared "soul root"). But most disciples were encouraged to content themselves with reaching the point on the Tree containing their past, present, and future selves, a sign that they had become *maskil* ("enlightened").

According to the Ari, only a handful of voyagers had penetrated the palaces leading to the Throne, which, he claimed, was another way of describing the highest spiritual experience occurring at the stage called Quarry of Souls. Joining the illustrious company of patriarchs, prophets, and Merkavah mystics who had accomplished this was like grasping one end of a bowed branch of the cosmic Tree. If a man could not generate enough spiritual power to hold fast, he could not count on the energy of his chosen sefirah to help him.

The Hasidim

If Isaac Luria was a lion to his Cubs, then Israel Baal Shem Tov, "Master of the Good Name," was a shepherd to his flock. The Ari soared to heaven and remained there, but it took the Baal Shem Tov to bring heaven back down to earth. The founder of modern Hasidism, Israel ben Eliezer of Miedzyboz (1700–1760), was "a man who lived with and for his fellow men on the foundation of his relation to the divine."[8] Born in 1700 around Okup in southern Poland, the Baal Shem Tov grew up as an orphan raised in foster homes. Unlike the well-off, scholarly Ari, the young Israel worked as a menial laborer, appearing to his neighbors as a kindly but ignorant fellow who loved children—a town fool of sorts. What the townsfolk didn't know was that the young village beadle, who swept the synagogue and led the children in dancing and singing on their way to school, was spending his nights meditating on the Lurianic Kabbalah in the synagogue basement.

It wasn't until Israel was slated to marry a distinguished local rabbi's daughter, against the wishes of her scholarly brother, Gershon Kitover, that the Baal Shem Tov revealed himself as a scriptural sage and spiritual master. One day, in a total public reversal, the illustrious Rabbi Gershon Kitover shocked the entire community by announcing that he had become the first disciple of the ragged

8. Buber, *Tales of the Hasidim: Early Masters*, p. 14.

synagogue beadle. That announcement marked the beginning of a new age of Jewish mystical companionship, which, unlike any of its predecessors, would spread beyond the confines of a "secret society" to circulate its teachings throughout the world.

Where the circle of ancient Merkavah initiates followed their masters through the complex maze of palaces leading to the heavenly Throne, and Abulafia's disciples looked to their teacher to unlock the secret codes hidden in the letters of the Torah, the Baal Shem Tov's Hasidim merely had to listen to him tell stories. Teaching his disciples how to understand the language of the birds, trees, animals, rocks, and stars, the founder of Hasidism disclosed the "secrets" of the Kabbalah.

The first group of Hasidim who gathered around the Baal Shem Tov included several men who would become great masters in their own right. Foremost of these was Dov Baer, the Maggid of Mezerich, a brilliant scriptural scholar turned itinerant preacher. Hearing of a wonder worker who he hoped would cure him of his chronic illness, the Maggid had wandered to the Baal Shem Tov's distant village. However, the initial meeting was a disappointment on all counts: not only couldn't the Baal Shem Tov cure the Maggid, but the supposed healer wasted his time chattering about his coachman's food preferences. Regretting that he'd come, the Maggid bade him farewell and returned to his inn. An hour or so later, there was a knock on the door, and the subject of the Baal Shem Tov's silly conversation, the coachman himself, was asking him to return. Apparently the Baal Shem Tov had something more to say. Reluctantly the Maggid returned to the healer's home, only to be tested on a difficult passage from the Lurianic Kabbalah. After delivering what he thought of as an impressive discourse, the Maggid waited for the Baal Shem Tov's response.

"You've learned only the body, not the soul," said the master. Then he proceeded to expound the passage himself.

Suffused by a sudden burst of warmth, the Maggid saw the entire room fill with a brilliant light that only faded when the Baal Shem Tov had stopped talking. Convinced that he had at last met his spiritual master, the Maggid remained at the Baal Shem Tov's side for the next twenty years and, at the founder's death, was designated his main successor.

The other masters emerging from the Baal Shem Tov's immediate circle were Pinchas of Koretz and Yechiel Mikhal of Zlotchov. But it was Dov Baer, the Great Maggid, as he was later called, who really functioned as the Baal Shem Tov's public voice. Although he was the most scholarly of the original disciples, the Maggid was best at translating the simplicity and spontaneity of his master's approach to the experience of No-thingness. To this end, he outlined an anthropomorphic portrait of humanity's relationship to God, describing it as reciprocal and intimate, and portraying God as teacher and humanity as disciple. Interestingly, the Maggid's own disciples each interpreted his teachings according to their own understanding. There was no insistence on common agreement, no right or wrong interpretation. The Maggid would simply make a suggestion or, following his master's example, tell a story, letting his Hasidim do with it as they saw fit. A famous example of this is the answer of one of his disciples, Rabbi Leib, to the question, "What did you learn at the Maggid's table?"

"I did not go to the Maggid in order to hear Torah from him, but to see how he unlaces his felt shoes and laces them up again."[9]

Another disciple, Rabbi Aaron of Karlin, responded to the same question by saying, "Nothing at all." Pressed further, Aaron said, "The nothing-at-all is what I learned. I learned the meaning of nothingness. I learned that I am nothing at all, and that I AM notwithstanding."[10]

Of the Maggid's three hundred disciples, forty became teachers

9. Buber, *Tales of the Hasidim: Early Masters*, p. 107.
10. Buber, *Tales of the Hasidim: Later Masters*, p. 8.

themselves. His grandson, Dov Baer of Lubavitch, was the most famous of these. The young Dov Baer's teaching style differed greatly
from that of his grandfather, however. Where the Maggid merely
threw out suggestions and allowed his Hasidim to "read" his mes-
sages for themselves, his Lubavitcher descendant strictly outlined
what he called the ten paths to ecstasy, which narrowly defined the
meditative way to No-thingness.

The second great teacher of the original circle, Rabbi Pinchas,
emphasized the experiential aspect of the Baal Shem Tov's teaching,
particularly the relationship between the inherent ecstasy of daily
life and No-thingness. Interweaving the emotional relationship to
God and its consequent effects on the seeker, Pinchas evolved "a
doctrine of dying and arising" which also demanded "sturdy living
in tune with all things of this earth, and a give-and-take community
with one's fellow men."[11]

The third teacher, Rabbi Yechiel, left a more ascetic legacy.
Brought to its fullest flower by his son, the gentle, compassionate
Zev Wolf of Zbarazh, Yechiel's teaching showered love on all Cre-
ation, encompassing sentient and insentient beings alike.

To avoid creating heretical cults like those of Sabbatai Zevi and
his ilk, the first generation of the Baal Shem Tov's disciples were very
careful not to declare themselves prophets or divine incarnations
who would usher in the Messianic Age. Therefore, the early Hasidic
teachers remained hidden at first, emerging only after they had been
designated by their teachers to carry on the tradition. If a leader died
without appointing a successor, then the community of mystical
companions elected one. Although later generations bestowed legendary status on the Baal Shem Tov, even he never proclaimed himself a tzaddik. The Maggid, too, strictly regarded himself as a
spiritual teacher. But by the nineteenth century, their successors
were fighting over questions of legitimacy, declaring bans and ex-

11. Buber, *Tales of the Hasidim: Later Masters*, p. 20.

communications against members of their own lineage, even prohibiting "intermarriage" between rival sects.

The resurgence of messianism is still the greatest issue dividing the Hasidim. Surfacing not long after the Maggid's death in the rivalry between the Seer of Lublin and Rabbi Yehudi of Pzhysha, the debate over the messiah's appearance at the End of Days continues to rage among the Lubavitchers and their opponents. Some Hasidim even regard contemporary political events, like Napoleon's conquest of Russia in the nineteenth century, and, in our own times, the creation of the State of Israel, as evidence for their claim. Yet, regardless of its position, no side in the dispute appears to remember why it began. More important, the rivals seem to be unaware of the yearning for union that brought them together as mystical companions in the first place.

4

Correspondences

The Ten Stages of Meditation

SINCE EVERY CREATED THING is a little universe in its own right and the goal of the mystic's life is to experience union with the Creator, a major part of the kabbalistic undertaking emphasizes meditation on the correspondences that link all Creation to the Source. Kabbalists discovered that using metaphors was the most economical way of communicating their instructions to those who had committed themselves to the spiritual path. Like poetry, the language of the mystics is, therefore, lyrical, condensed, and often hard to understand at first glance. Similarly designed to communicate subjective experience rather than convey facts, kabbalistic imagery requires both literal and figurative translation. This is especially important in tracing the variety of expressions that characterize the ten basic stages of meditation symbolized by the sefirot and their analogues.

> *First Stage: Ein (No-Thing)*
> Emanation: Yesh (Being emerges out of No-thing.)
> Sefirah: Keter
> Hebrew Letter: Alef

Soul Level: Ruach
Angel: Metatron

Presupposing that the aspirant has developed the highest level of concentration (the realm of no-thought) available to spiritual consciousness (ruach), meditation on Ein deemphasizes visualization and focuses primarily on the breath as the purest emanation of Being. The white sefirah Keter corresponds to the white matter in the brain, which, directly linked to the meditator's inhalations and exhalations, is the first manifestation of consciousness, exemplified by the first letter, Alef. Metatron, the sword-wielding guardian of the Throne, represents unfaltering kavvanah without a trace of thought.

Second Stage: Consciousness

Emanation: Knowing
Sefirah: Chokhmah
Hebrew Letter: Bet
Soul Level: Ruach
Angel: Raziel

At this stage of meditation, consciousness corresponds to union with the Beloved in the same way that lovers, in biblical terminology, sexually "know" each other. Bound to God, manifesting as the Wisdom symbolized by the sefirah Chokhmah, the aspirant who achieves this stage of meditation is at the threshold of thought, a lower level of ruach than that represented by Keter. The Hebrew letter Bet corresponds to "building a house" (constructing thoughts), an activity overseen by the protector of the home, the angel Raziel.

Third Stage: Intellect

Emanation: Thinking
Sefirah: Binah

Hebrew Letter: Gimel
Soul Level: Ruach
Angel: Zafkiel

One must develop a strong, well-balanced mind if one is not to be frightened off by the vast energy of creative forces at work in the universe, here personified by the angel Zafkiel. In the primordial realm of as yet undifferentiated thought, the power of Gimel, the third letter in the Hebrew alphabet, is reflected in the harmonized body, mind, and spirit of the meditator. In this condition, one is prepared to understand the mystery of the unity of all things, the experience imparted by Binah.

Fourth Stage: Purity
Emanation: Righteousness
Sefirah: Chesed
Hebrew Letter: Dalet
Soul Level: Neshamah
Angel: Tzadkiel

Forming a pillar between heaven and earth, the righteous person inhabits the highly developed moral consciousness that characterizes both the sefirah Chesed and the spiritually developed human soul. Righteousness is here embodied by the angel Tzadkiel, whose name shares the same root as the word *tzaddik*, righteous one. Since purity, in the form of selflessness, pervades such a person's every word and deed, the righteous serve as vehicles for the divine will. For them, meditation is effortless; their very existence in the world provides an open door, in the form of the letter Dalet, through which others may pass.

Fifth Stage: Differentiation
Emanation: Discipline
Sefirah: Gevurah
Hebrew Letter: Heh

Soul Level: Neshamah
Angel: Samael

Like Metatron, who is also depicted holding a sword, the angel Samael embodies the power to discipline the erratic mind. The difference between them is that Samael, who is lower in the angelic hierarchy, rules the dualistic realm. Aligned with Gevurah and the letter Heh, whose numerical equivalent is 5 (corresponding to the five fingers of the hand), this stage of meditation represents discipline (taking oneself in hand) and is emblematic of the quiet strength and patience born of the knowledge of right and wrong.

Sixth Stage: Being
Emanation: Subjectivity
Sefirah: Tiferet
Hebrew Letter: Vav
Soul Level: Neshamah
Angel: Mikhael (Michael)

At this level of meditation, the aspirant occupies the higher realm of subjectivity, the stage of neshamah at which one begins to distinguish between self and other. Identified with Mikhael, the guardian of the community of Israel, the abode of Shekhinah, and the sefirah Tiferet, one regards oneself as an individual, touched by, yet distinct from, the divine source of one's being. Shaped like a plumb-line with a hook at the top, the letter Vav represents the link between the contemplative and the object of contemplation.

Seventh Stage: Energy
Emanation: Control
Sefirah: Netzach
Hebrew Letter: Zayin
Soul Level: Nefesh
Angel: Haniel

Nefesh, the instinctual, or material, soul is the interface between the spiritual and physical realms. At this level of concentration, the meditator must exert control over the powerful energy generated by the mind. To avert the danger of giving way to strong emotions or hallucinations, this stage of meditation is accompanied by the letter Zayin, in the shape of a walking stick or prop for the perilous journey. Often manifesting as a maggid, the angel Haniel functions as a guide rather than as a guardian barring the meditator's path.

Eighth Stage: Communication

Emanation: Listening
Sefirah: Hod
Hebrew Letter: Chet
Soul Level: Nefesh
Angel: Refael (Raphael)

Characterized by the Maggid of Mezerich as the *universe of listening*—a condition in which the self is dissolved until one is nothing but an ear reverberating with sound—this stage of meditation represents the highest form of sensory absorption in the instinctual soul of nefesh. Hod is the nexus between the senses and their objects of perception. The letter Chet, open at the base, symbolizes the open ear, alert to the sounds of the world. Refael is the messenger who calls attention to the still, small voice of God that echos throughout Creation.

Ninth Stage: Structure

Emanation: Support
Sefirah: Yesod
Hebrew Letter: Tet
Soul Level: Nefesh
Angel: Gavriel (Gabriel)

Gavriel represents the opportunity to dissolve the ego in oneness with God. The angel serves as a monitor, reminding the aspirant of the divine support that is manifest in the structure of the human form itself. Yesod is the ground of human experience, the mid-level of nefesh, symbolizing a field that is rich in possibilities for forgetting the self in everyday activities. The letter Tet (whose numerical equivalent is 9, relating it to the mystical "enneagram") symbolizes the successful completion of a structure.

Tenth Stage: Feeling

Emanation: Devotion
Sefirah: Malkhut
Hebrew Letter: Yod
Soul Level: Nefesh
Angel: Sandalfon

Malkhut is the sefirah of desires and feelings that impel action. The desire that drives the aspirant to take the arduous path to oneness is devotion, a spiritual passion that corresponds to falling in love. At this level, the instinctual soul is synonymous with the vital rush of feeling that accompanies the discovery of the existence of the Beloved. Sandalfon is the angel of revelation, allowing the lover a glimpse behind the illusory curtain of separation. The letter Yod, an abbreviated version of the letter Vav—the bridge between subject and object—holds out the promise of union.

The Faces of God

THE HOLY ANCIENT ONE

A vivid, anthropomorphic group of images for meditation described in the *Zohar* focuses on the *partzufim*, faces of God. Divided into three aspects that correspond to the divine emanations and the archetypal worlds of the Tree of Life, the partzufim represent the transmutation of the Divine No-thing into form. The very first of these emanations, residing in Ein Sof, is unseen. It represents the stage of meditation where "face did not gaze upon face," that is, consciousness devoid of thought.

Corresponding to meditation on the emanations symbolized by the sefirot Keter, Chokhmah, Binah, Chesed, Gevurah, Tiferet, Netzach, and Hod that reside in the archetypal world of Atzilut is the face called the Holy Ancient One. Its features are visualized as a skull (Keter), the white matter of the brain inside the skull (Chokhmah), an airy membrane covering the brain (Binah), a beard consisting of white wool (Chesed), a forehead synonymous with power (Gevurah), an open eye that stands for unfaltering attention (Tiferet), and the nostrils and nose that contain the life breath of all that exists (Netzach and Hod).

Residing in the archetypal world of Beriah are the seven lower sefirot, personified by the facial features of the Holy Ancient One. These correspond to the seven Hebrew words of the first verse of Genesis, whose permuted letters simultaneously represent the energies inherent in Creation and the stages of meditation encoded in Genesis. In a section called "The Book of Concealment," the *Zohar* points out that, excluding the first word, the second verse of Genesis consists of thirteen Hebrew words, each of which embodies a meditative variation on Chesed. Together, these are called the thirteen paths of mercy in the beard of the Ancient One. Aligned with these are the letters Yod, Heh, Vav, Heh, which correspond, respectively, to Chokhmah, the Father; Binah, the Mother (also known as the Upper Shekhinah); and the Small Face, which includes the final Heh and corresponds to the Lower Shekhinah. Hidden between the Yod and the first Heh is a tongue that stands for the secret sefirah Daat, the key to knowledge of the six sefirot that make up the Small Face.

Taken together, the partzufim and sefirot form a meditative blueprint that begins at the highest level of nonthought and ends in a return to ordinary consciousness. The skull containing the white matter corresponds to the most advanced stage of kavvanah, where the boundaries between subject and object are dissolved. Focused meditation is represented by the ability to traverse the paths of consciousness (beard) while fully awake (the open eye) and attending to the breath (nostrils and nose). The time of day indicated for performing this meditation on Chesed is contained in the assertion that the thirteen paths of the beard "establish themselves in mercy and renew themselves in the early morning."[1]

Instructions for breathing and permuting the letters of the Tetragrammaton accompany the meditation. Recitation of the first Heh emphasizes the exhaled breath, in the same way that the Ancient One breathes life into the Creation, which is symbolized by the six sefirot in the form of the Small Face. Unifying the two Hehs, or "balancing" the Yod, Heh, and Vav, means that the meditator must hold the exhaled breath after reciting each letter.

THE SMALL FACE

The *Zohar* also provides explicit instructions for meditation on the nine paths of the beard of the Small Face, which correspond to the nine sefirot emanating from Keter. One visualizes oneself traveling through the hairs of the beard, beginning at the temples, moving to the top of the mouth, through the moustache, chin, and downward to the throat. En route, there are references to the feminine red cheeks and lips of the face, and an allusion to the strength provided to those who can locate themselves in the perfectly balanced, symmetrical rows of tresses (maintain perfect concentration). The journey described here is actually a meditation on the female sefirah Gevurah (red), visualized as the androgynous face of Adam Kadmon. It is affiliated with the sacred Name Elohim, and is designed to harmonize one's masculine and feminine qualities.

1. Roy A. Rosenberg, *The Anatomy of God.* (New York: Ktav Publishing House, 1973), p. 16.

Where the Ancient One is beyond imagining, the Small Face is accessible through visualization and letter permutation. However, by combining meditation on the sefirot and their affiliated Names, and thereby balancing the conflicting material and spiritual forces personified by the "lower" Adam (the dualistic mind) and Adam Kadmon (the unified spirit), one can progress to the hidden realm of the Ancient One (nonthought). The *Zohar's* discussion of the journey through the beard of the Small Face assures us that the hidden Ancient One will be revealed to those who meditate according to its instructions. Serious aspirants are encouraged not to stop until they realize that the Ancient One and the Small Face are really one and the same.

The Tetragrammaton

The Hebrew words *Bereshit bara*—"In the beginning He created" (Genesis 1:1)—open the ten utterances by which God created the worlds. According to the *Zohar*, *Bereshit* is a complete statement, while *bara* constitutes only half a statement, indicating that God is simultaneously hidden and revealed (the Ancient One and the Small Face). Like the gap between the instinctual and spiritual soul in human beings, the separation between the partzufim is only apparent. The two are really one. Only by emulating the Ancient One ("My breath will not restrict itself within the higher Adam") and breathing life into the Names associated with each of the ten sayings (the sefirot) can the devotee breach the apparent gap between matter and spirit. Located in the Small Face (the physical body), one literally creates oneself anew with every breath. Here, the reference to Creation stands for a brief meditation on the Name Yah (using Yod, the first letter of the Tetragrammaton), which is accompanied by a mental recitation of the Name, an inhalation through the nose and an exhalation through the mouth.

Meditation on Heh (the second letter of the Tetragrammaton) is performed by mentally reciting the article *ha* ("the") from the word *ha-adam*, the androgynous earthly Adam. Described as "the blowing of the wind over all," this technique involves vehemently expelling the breath through the mouth and holding the exhalation while visualizing Malkhut in the form of the Divine Mother.

Identified with the Small Face, the letter Vav is the subject of a visualization technique known as "the dark lamp." Using the Vav as a chisel, the meditator captures a spark of light from the realm of the Ancient One, hews it to form the skull of the Small Face, then fills in the paths of the beard. The letter Vav represents the link between the upper sefirot and the six emanations corresponding to the six days of creation, and the male aspect of the Ancient One. It is identified with the "planting of the Garden" described in the second chapter of Genesis and stands for human activity. The Vav symbolizes the unification of above and below when one applies kavvanah to all one's worldly tasks.

The final Heh stands for *Hu*, the transcendent Ancient One. Unification with this hidden face can only be accomplished by one who has advanced through the stage of meditation on the first Heh to the point where the Ancient One reveals itself. It cannot be sought after, but occurs naturally to the one who is prepared for the experience.

Creation

Ma'aseh Bereshit (Tales of Creation), an eighth-century text, provides instructions for meditation that correspond to the six days of Creation. Although it is hidden under a dense layer of esoteric iconography and letter permutations, those who can decipher the code will immediately recognize Tales of Creation as a variation on a familiar theme. Each "day" (meditation) is represented by a stage in the creation process, a sefirah and its accompanying color, a direction, and a set of letters for permutation. On the appropriate day of the week, and facing the proper direction, one visualizes the assigned sefirah while mentally permuting the letters and chanting the re-formulated Names. (See table 3, pages 88–89.)

The seventh day, the Sabbath, is the occasion for unifying Yesod (male) and Malkhut (female). Designated as "The Streams that Sing," this meditation is represented by the Sabbath liturgy, sung with kavvanah, that simultaneously exalts the Shekhinah and brings about the unification of the upper and lower waters (masculine and feminine polarities). Afforded an extra soul on this day, the Kabbalist is bound to the Beloved. This means that one remains in a medita-tive state from the moment the Shekhinah (spirit) enters the house (the body), thus completing the cycle of Creation.

Measuring the Body

A complex form of meditation that combines visualization and letter permutation, Measuring the Body offers little room for distrac-tion. Although it demands complete familiarity with the sacred Names, numbers, and features associated with the cosmic form of Adam Kadmon, this technique has long served as an effective man-dala for inducing focused concentration. Described in the eleventh-century meditation manual *Shiur Komah*, the experience is similar to the Tibetan *nöndro* practice, an esoteric meditation technique involving daily chanting and the performance of more than 200,000 prostrations over the course of several months or years. Related to the meditation on the partzufim, where one travels through the paths of the cosmic beard, Measuring the Body consists of visualizing oneself on a journey from the soles of the feet to the top of the head of the cosmic body of Adam Kadmon while permuting the sacred Names (letters and numbers) that correspond to the divine manifes-tations encountered at each stage of meditation. Meditators were obviously not expected to perform all of these visualizations, but rather to focus exclusively on one over a period of months or years. (See table 4, pages 92–100.)

The Throne

A related set of visualizations corresponds to the composition of the cosmic Throne (table 5, page 101). Permuting letters taken from phrases in the Torah, Kabbalists constructed imagined tapestries of fantastic beasts and angelic beings that sprang to life with their recitations. One of the most frequently recurring of these visualizations depicts the Throne of Glory on which Adam Kadmon is seated. Its name is made up of the letters Lamed, Vav, Resh, Kaf, Zayin, Peh, Yod, Resh, Vav, Tav, and Alef. Its feet are actually living beings, *Chayyot* (sing. *Chayyah*), whose respective names are Aglav, Babak, Kabab, and Azbya. The four faces and four wings of the Chayyot symbolize the levels of the human soul (stages of meditation) and, in addition to being subjects for visualization, function as letters and numbers for permutation that are personified as angelic guardians. Each Chayyah contains four faces that are attached at each corner to four wings, which themselves are attached to four wings, giving a total of sixty-four wings to each Chayyah.

The Heavenly Chamber

A host of celestial colors, sounds, sensations, and images corresponds to the physical sensations encountered on the journey through the heavenly chamber where the Throne is located. Depicted as a "field of herbs," the ground in front of the Throne represents the incense, herbs, or pinch of snuff used to relax the body and quiet the mind. Chanting the name Arafel, the meditator at first discerns the image of Adam Kadmon surrounded by a thick dark cloud. But as concentration deepens, one begins to make out discrete images. Chanting the words "Mighty and Strong" and visualiz-

Table 3. The Six Days of Creation

First Day: Creating Heaven and Earth
Sefirah: Keter
Color: White
Direction: North
Letters for Permutation:
  Alef-Lamed-Alef-Lamed
  Alef-Lamed-Bet-Yod-Mem
  Bet-Lamed-Yod-Alef-Lamed
  Bet-Lamed-Yod
  Bet-Samech-Lamed-Yod-Alef

Second Day: Separating the Waters
Sefirah: Chokhmah
Color: Blue
Direction: South
Letters for Permutation:
  Dalet-Resh-Nun-Yod-Alef-Lamed
  Dalet-Resh-Kaf-Yod-Alef-Lamed
  Heh-Mem-Vav-Nun-Yod-Alef-Lamed
  Gimel-Heh-Nun-Yod-Alef-Lamed

Third Day: Planting a Garden
Sefirah: Binah
Color: Green
Direction: East
Letters for Permutation:
  Dalet-Vav-Resh-Nun-Yod-Alef-Lamed
  Gimel-Bet-Resh-Yod-Alef-Lamed
  Gimel-Dalet-Resh-Yod-Alef-Lamed
  Ayin-Dalet-Resh-Yod-Alef-Lamed
  Mem-Vav-Dalet-Yod-Alef-Lamed
  Resh-Heh-Mem-Yod-Alef-Lamed
  Heh-Nun-Yod-Alef-Lamed

Fourth Day: Creating the Sun and the Moon

Sefirot: Chesed and Gevurah

Colors: White and Red

Direction: West

Letters for Permutation:
    Yod-Alef-Lamed-Samech-Nun
    Samech-Vav-Kaf-Yod-Alef-Lamed
    Tzade-Nun-Samech-Yod-Alef-Lamed
    Bet-Kaf-Tav-Mem-Yod-Alef-Lamed
    Tav-Resh-Peh-Nun-Yod-Alef-Lamed

Fifth Day: The Living Waters

Sefirah: Tiferet

Color: White

Direction: South

Letters for Permutation:
    Tav-Yod-Alef-Lamed
    Ayin-Nun-Yod-Alef-Lamed
    Nun-Nun-Alef-Lamed
    Heh-Lamed-Kaf-Yod-Mem
    Heh-Nun-Yod-Alef-Lamed

Sixth Day: Living Souls

Sefirot: Netzach and Hod

Colors: Red and Green

Direction: East

Letters for Permutation:
    Mem-Samech-Yod-Mem
    Chet-Resh-Mem-Yod-Alef-Lamed

ing oneself in the form of a young man who prostrates himself before the Throne (Metatron), the meditator permutes the letters that constitute the sacred Names Alef-Heh-Heh; Yod-Heh-Vav-Heh; Yod-Heh-Vav; Heh-Vav; Heh-Vav; Yod-Vav-Heh-Vav; Yod-Heh-Yod-Yod-Heh.

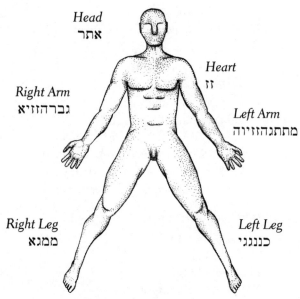

FIGURE 4. The cosmic body of Adam Kadmon, showing a few of the correspondences and letters of permutation. (See table 4.)

The permutations are recited in a "roar" of fire and hail, an allusion to the vigorous breathing techniques accompanying the process. Led by the meditator in the form of Metatron, hosts of angels join the chanting as the permutations speed up and grow more complex. The cosmic man himself appears in the form of a consuming fire that assumes the shapes of the letters of the name Adam (Alef-Dalet-Mem). Using the first letter, the meditator permutes the Name into Alef-Heh-Yod-Heh; Alef-Shin-Resh; Alef-Heh-Yod-Heh (I Am That Which Is and Always Will Be) and recites it seven times.

One next visualizes the Throne surrounded by angels and Chayyot, as the Shekhinah manifests herself at the center. Assuming a breathy whisper (the still, small voice), the meditator announces, "This is the Throne of Glory." Afterward, everything grows silent; the angels are consumed by the holy fire; the Chayyot prostrate themselves and put their faces to the ground; the sound of the fire (breath) grows audible as the meditator (still in the person of Meta-tron) chants the permutations on the Name of Glory:

Alef-Dalet-Resh-Yod-Heh-Vav
Alef-Heh-Resh-Kaf-Yod
Heh-Heh-Yod-Yod
Yod-Heh-Vav-Heh
Alef-Heh-Yod-Heh-Alef-Shin-Resh-Alef-Heh-Yod-Heh
Heh-Heh-Yod
Yod-Vav-Alef
Heh-Kaf-Heh
Heh-Heh
Vav-Heh
Heh-Vav-Heh
Vav-Heh-Vav
Heh-Heh
Heh-Yod-Alef
Heh-Vav-Alef
Heh-Heh
Yod-Heh-Yod-Heh-Yod
Heh-Yod
Yod-Heh-Yod-Heh
Yod-Heh-Vav-Heh

The meditation ends with a song of praise and a recitation of the 93rd, 29th, and 24th Psalms.

Table 4. Measuring the Body

1

Visualization: Sole of Right Foot

Letters for Permutation:
 Peh-Resh-Sof-Mem-Yod-Alef
 Alef-Tav-Resh-Kaf-Tet-Tet

Numbers for Permutation: 300,000 (Append Shin to each letter and recite 1,000 times.)

Toes of Right Foot

Letters for Permutation:
 Alef-Tet-Resh-Mem-Zayin
 Alef-Dalet-Resh-Mem-Tet
 Bet-Resh-Mem-Nun-Mem
 Bet-Resh-Tav-Heh-Mem-Yod-Mem
 Vav-Alef-Heh-Vav-Zayin

Numbers for Permutation: 100,000 (Append Kaf to each letter and recite 100,000 times.)

2

Visualization: Sole of Left Foot

Letters for Permutation: Alef-Gimel-Tav-Mem-Nun

Numbers for Permutation: 300,000 (Append Shin to each letter and recite 1,000 times.)

Toes of Left Foot

Letters for Permutation:
 Zayin-Kaf-Yod-Yod-Nun
 Kaf-Zayin-Kof-Yod-Yod-Nun
 Heh-Tet-Mem-Tet

Numbers for Permutation: 100,000 (Append Kaf to each letter and recite 100,000 times.)

3

Visualization: Right Ankle

Letters for Permutation:
 Tzade-Nun-Mem-Tet-Nun-Yod-Heh
 Tav-Samech-Samech-Kaf-Mem

Numbers for Permutation: 10,000 (Append letter Yod to each letter and recite 10,000 times.)

4

Visualization: Right Leg
Letters for Permutation:
  Mem-Mem-Gimel-Alef
  Vav-Zayin-Vav-Yod-Alef
Numbers for Permutation: 19,004 (Append letters Yod and Tet to each
  letter and recite 19,004 times.)

5

Visualization: Left Leg
Letters for Permutation:
  Kaf-Nun-Nun-Gimel-Gimel-Yod
  Mem-Heh-Resh-Yod-Heh
  Tav-Samech-Samech-Kaf-Vav-Mem
Numbers for Permutation: 19,004 (Append letters Yod and Tet to each
  letter and recite 19,004 times.)

6

Visualization: Right Thigh
Letters for Permutation:
  Samech-Samech-Peh-Vav-Samech-Tet
  Peh-Resh-Samech-Bet
Numbers for Permutation: 134,000 (Append letters Kaf, Lamed, and
  Dalet to each letter and recite 134,000 times.)

7

Visualization: Left Thigh
Letters for Permutation:
  Mem-Mem-Gimel-Alef
  Vav-Zayin-Vav-Yod-Alef
Numbers for Permutation: 134,000 (Append letters Kaf, Lamed, and
  Dalet to each letter and recite 134,000 times.)

8

Visualization: Torso

Loins
Letters for Permutation:
  Mem-Vav-Tet-Nun-Yod-Heh-Vav
  Alef-Tav-Samech-Gimel-Heh
  Yod-Dalet-Yod-Dalet-Yod-Heh

Table 4. (*continued*)

Numbers for Permutation: 34,010 (Append letters Lamed, Dalet, and
  Yod to each letter and recite 34,010 times.)

Heart
Letters for Permutation:
  Zayin-Zayin
  Tzade-Dalet-Kaf (Tzaddik = Righteous)
  Tzade-Heh-Yod-Ayin-Lamed
  Tzade-Vav-Resh (Zur = Rock)
  Tzade-Bet-Yod
  Tzade-Dalet-Yod-Kaf (Tzaddik = Righteous)
  Kaf-Alef-Peh
  Samech-Resh-Alef-Peh
  Bet-Vav-Heh-Nun
  Tzade-Bet-Alef-Vav-Tav (Tzevaot = Hosts)
  Shin-Dalet-Ein (Shaddai)
  Alef-Lamed-Heh-Yod-Mem (Elohim)
  Yod-Heh-Vav-Heh-Yod (Shem Ha-m'foresh)
  Tzade-Yod (white)
  Dalet-Gimel-Vav-Lamed (Dagul = distinguished)
  Vav-Dalet-Vav-Mem (Vadom = red)
  Samech-Samech-Samech
  Alef-Alef-Alef
  Alef-Alef-Alef
  Alef-Yod-Alef
  Alef-Heh-Vav
  Resh-Bet-Yod-Heh
  Heh-Heh
  Heh-Vav
  Vav-Heh
  Tzade-Tzade-Tzade
  Peh-Peh-Peh
  Kaf-Nun
  Heh-Heh
  Heh-Yod
  Heh-Yod
  Heh-Yod

Resh Vav-Kaf-Bet (Rokhev = horseman)
Alef-Resh-Bet-Vav-Tav (Arabot = heaven)
Yod-Heh (first half of Shem Ha-m'foresh)
Mem-Mem-Mem
Nun-Nun-Nun
Heh-Vav-Vav
Yod-Heh
Heh-Peh-Tzade (Shem ha-Fetz)
Heh-Zayin-Zayin
Alef-Yod
Zayin-Alef
Tet-Alef-Alef
Alef-Alef-Alef
Kaf-Kaf-Kaf (Kadosh, Kadosh, Kadosh = Holy, Holy, Holy)
Kaf-Shin-Resh (Kesher)
Resh-Zayin (Raz = concealed)
Zayin-Kaf (Zak = pure)
Gimel-Bet-Vav-Resh (Gibor = powerful)
Yod-Alef
Yod-Alef
Yod-Vav-Dalet
Heh-Alef-Nun
Alef-Lamed-Peh (Alef = primordial source of being)
Dalet-Yod-Mem-Nun
Peh-Alef-Peh
Kaf-Vav-Peh
Resh-Alef-Peh
Yod-Yod-Yod
Yod-Yod-Alef
Kaf-Kaf-Bet
Tav-Tav-Tav
Bet-Kaf-Kaf
Peh-Lamed-Lamed
Samech-Yod-Yod-Mem
Concludes with the recitation: Barukh Shem Kavod Malkhuto, Le'olam
  Va-ed (Blessed be the Name of the glory of His Kingdom forever)
Numbers for Permutation: 70 (Append Ayin to each letter and recite 70
  times.)

TABLE 4. *(continued)*

Right Shoulder
Letters for Permutation:
   Mem-Tav-Tav-Gimel-Resh-Yod-Alef-Alef
   Alef-Nun-Gimel-Nun
Numbers for Permutation: 16,000 (Append Yod, Heh, and Alef to each
   letter and recite 16,000 times.)

Left Shoulder
Letters for Permutation:
   Tet-Tet-Mem-Heh-Yod-Nun-Tet-Alef
   Samech-Lamed-Mem-Heh
   Yod-Nun-Nun-Yod-Ayin-Lamed
Numbers for Permutation: 16,000 (Append Yod, Heh, and Alef to each
   letter and recite 16,000 times.)

Right Arm
Letters for Permutation:
   Gimel-Bet-Resh-Heh-Zayin-Zayin-Yod-Alef
   Alef-Kaf-Bet-Vav-Yod
Numbers for Permutation: 16,000 (Append Yod, Heh, and Alef to each
   letter and recite 16,000 times.)

Left Arm
Letters for Permutation:
   Mem-Tav-Tav-Gimel-Heh-Zayin-Zayin-Yod-Vav-Heh
Numbers for Permutation: 16,000 (Append Yod, Heh, and Alef to each
   letter and recite 16,000 times.)

Each Finger of Right Hand
Letters for Permutation:
   Tav-Tav-Mem-Zayin-Mem-Zayin
   Gimel-Gimel-Mem-Vav-Tav
   Gimel-Gimel-Samech-Mem-Samech
Numbers for Permutation: 25,000 (Append Kaf and Heh to each letter
   and recite 25,000 times.)

Each Finger of Left Hand
Letters for Permutation: Alef-Shin-Vav-Zayin-Yod-Heh

Numbers for Permutation: 25,000 (Append Kaf and Heh to each letter and recite 25,000 times.)

Palm of Right Hand
Letters for Permutation:
  Heh-Zayin-Zayin-Yod-Alef
  Alef-Tet-Gimel-Resh-Yod-Yod-Alef
Numbers for Permutation: 14,000 (Append Yod and Dalet to each letter and recite 14,000 times.)

Palm of Left Hand
Letters for Permutation: Alef-Samech-Heh-Vav-Zayin-Yod-Heh
Numbers for Permutation: 14,000 (Append Yod and Dalet to each letter and recite 14,000 times.)

9
Visualization: Neck
Letters for Permutation:
  Samech-Nun-Nun-Yod-Heh-Vav
  Vav-Bet-Heh-Tav-Yod-Kaf-Nun
Numbers for Permutation: 23,800 (Append letters Kaf, Gimel, and final Peh to each letter and recite 23,800 times.)

10
Visualization: Head
Letters for Permutation:
  Alef-Tav-Resh
  Heh-Vav-Dalet-Resh-Yod-Heh
  Alef-Tav-Samech-Yod-Heh
  Alef-Tav-Tav-Yod-Heh
Numbers for Permutation: 310,033⅓ (Append letters Shin, Lamed, and Gimel to each letter and recite 310,033⅓ times.)

11
Visualization: Beard
Letters for Permutation:
  Heh-Dalet-Resh-Resh-Kof
  Samech-Mem-Yod-Alef

T ABLE 4. (*continued*)

Numbers for Permutation: 11,500 (Append letters Yod, Alef, and final Kaf to each letter and recite 11,500 times.)

12
Visualization: Nose
Letters for Permutation:
  Lamed-Gimel-Bet-Tav-Yod-Yod-Alef
  Alef-Bet-Resh-Gimel-Gimel
  Tav-Tav-Peh-Yod-Yod-Heh
Numbers for Permutation: None

13
Visualization: Lips

Upper Lip
Letters for Permutation:
  Gimel-Bet-Resh-Heh
  Tav-Yod-Alef
Numbers for Permutation: 77 (Append Ayin and Zayin to each letter and recite 77 times.)

Lower Lip
Letters for Permutation: Heh-Zayin-Resh-Gimel-Yod-Alef
Numbers for Permutation: 77 (Append Ayin and Zayin to each letter and recite 77 times.)

14
Visualization: Tongue
Letters for Permutation:
  Alef-Samech-Samech-Gimel-Yod-Yod-Heh-Vav
  Vav-Alef-Yod-Yod-Alef
Numbers for Permutation: None

15
Visualization: Forehead
Letters for Permutation:
  Yod-Yod-Heh-Vav
  Heh-Heh
  Yod-Vav-Heh
  Vav-Yod-Heh

Heh-Alef
Heh-Yod
Heh-Yod
Heh-Yod
Heh-Alef
Heh-Heh
Vav-Vav-Heh
Yod-Yod-Yod
Heh-Vav
Vav-Yod-Heh-Vav
Heh-Heh
Yod-Heh
Alef-Yod
Heh-Heh
Yod-Heh
Yod-Heh
Yod-Alef
Heh-Vav
Heh-Vav
Yod-Yod-Heh-Yod-Yod
Heh-Yod-Heh
Yod-Heh-Vav
Heh-Samech
Heh-Alef
Heh-Yod-Heh
Vav-Yod-Heh
Numbers for Permutation: None

16
Visualization: Pupil of Right Eye (Black)
Letters for Permutation:
Alef-Zayin-Resh-Yod-Yod-Heh
Alef-Tet-Tet-Yod-Tet-Vav-Samech (Rehevel = master of clear vision)[2]

2. Because techniques for permuting the Hebrew letters vary among Kabbalistic texts, the names of angelic guardians do not always correspond to the letters emerging from the permutations, nor do the letters necessarily form recognizable words or phrases. Syntax and consistency are less important than breaking down phrases and letters into pure sound. Visualizations are similarly meant to be dissolved into formless "No-thingness."

TABLE 4. (*continued*)

Numbers for Permutation: 11,500 (Append letters Yod, Alef, and final
   Kaf to each letter and recite 11,500 times.)

17
Visualization: Pupil of Left Eye (Black)
Letters for Permutation:
   Mem-Tet-Tet
   Gimel-Resh-Vav-Peh-Mem-Zayin-Yod-Alef
Numbers for Permutation: 11,500 (Append letters Yod, Alef, and final
   Kaf to each letter and recite 11,500 times.)

18
Visualization: White of Right Eye
Letters for Permutation: Bet-Zayin-Kaf-Vav-Heh-Alef
Numbers for Permutation: 222,002 (Append letters Resh, Kaf, and Bet
   to each letter and recite 222,002 times.)

19
Visualization: White of Left Eye
Letters for Permutation: Bet-Zayin-Kaf-Vav-Heh-Alef
Numbers for Permutation: 222,002 (Append letters Resh, Kaf, and Bet
   to each letter and recite 222,002 times.)

20
Visualization: Ears

Right Ear
Letters for Permutation: Alef-Zayin-Tet-Heh-Yod-Yod-Alef
Numbers for Permutation: None

Left Ear
Letters for Permutation: Mem-Nun-Vav-Gimel-Heh-Vav
Numbers for Permutation: None

FIGURE 5. The four Chayyot: Lion, Eagle, Ox, and Man.

TABLE 5. The Cosmic Throne

First Face: Lion = Ruach

Angelic Guardian: Heh-Vav-Dalet-Vav-Dalet-Yod-Heh-Heh-Yod-Dalet-Vav-
Alef-Heh-Alef-Lamed-Alef-Vav-Resh-Yod-Alef-Heh-Vav-Dalet-Heh-Vav-
Yod-Heh-Tet-Mem-Gimel-Mem-Zayin
Number for Permutation: 4

Second Face: Eagle = Neshamah

Angelic Guardian: Alef-Peh-Peh-Yod-Alef-Lamed-Yod-Heh-Mem-Mem-
Zayin-Yod-Tav-Zayin-Heh-Vav-Resh-Yod-Resh-Yod-Alef-Lamed
Number for Permutation: 4

Third Face: Ox = Nefesh

Angelic Guardian: Samech-Vav-Resh-Heh-Lamed-Yod-Heh-Zayin-Mem-
Zayin-Mem-Mem-Kaf-Alef-Mem-Samech-Kaf-Yod-Alef
Number for Permutation: 4

Fourth Face: Man = Instinctual level of Nefesh

Angelic Guardian: Alef-Lamed-Yod-Heh-Alef-Mem-Zayin-Bet-Alef-Mem-
Zayin-Alef-Mem-Tav-Kaf-Mem-Zayin
Number for Permutation: 4

5
Kabbalah and Everyday Life

Raising the Sparks

SINCE THE DAYS OF Rabbi Akiva, Kabbalists have placed the greatest emphasis on experiencing God in daily life. With a few exceptions, Jewish mystics were constantly warned against asceticism, particularly when it came to separating spiritual practice from the body and its functions. Indeed, as the very image of the Divine, the human form is regarded as godly, to be treated as a dwelling place for Shekhinah. Thus, every moment of the seeker's life provides him or her with an opportunity for recalling the sanctity of all created things. There are meditative moments for all of life's activities, from waking in the morning, going to the bathroom, fixing and eating breakfast, to interacting with one's colleagues at work around the coffee wagon.

Moses Cordovero phrased the preceding sentences in more religious-sounding terms, but he was basically saying the same thing when he told his students that "the essence of the divine image is action. What good is it if your anatomy corresponds to the supernal form, while your actions do not resemble God's? So imitate the acts of Keter, the thirteen qualities of compassion . . . you should desire

102

the well-being of your fellow creature . . . for you and your fellow are one and the same."[1]

Cordovero then goes on to provide a set of exercises using the various parts of the body that correspond to the divine emanations on the cosmic Tree. Moving from the brain to the eyes, ears, nose, and mouth, he advocates using the sensory apparatus as a means for dropping the ego and experiencing oneself as No-thing, and then enjoins his students to use these personal daily meditations to inform their social behavior. Teaching others by example, each according to his or her capacity, one must mindfully return to Binah, the sefirah of Understanding, and remain rooted there. Even flawed thoughts and deeds, Cordovero assures us, can be transformed through the constant practice of meditation. At the same time, because all Creation is interconnected, such concentrated individual effort will serve to spread harmony and compassion throughout the universe.

The *Zohar* similarly enjoins Kabbalists to meditate on Chokhmah, the sefirah of Wisdom, in order to facilitate the descent of the spiritualizing power of Shekhinah into every human soul.

One should not take *soul* here as referring to a physical entity that transmigrates through the sefirotic worlds along the Tree. Rather, Moses de Leon was presenting philosophical concepts by using traditional kabbalistic metaphors that, though immediately recognizable to his peers, he knew would not be taken literally. When he says that the spiritual nature of the soul comes from the sefirah of Chokhmah, Wisdom, he is talking about that aspect of the human mind that possesses the capacity to experience No-thingness. It is to this end that all meditation, prayer, and daily activity are directed. Over and over again, the flawed self must repair the apparent breach between No-thing and the world of things. And our life in this world is the vehicle for doing so. Isaac Luria framed it in an even more worldly

---

1. Quoted in Matt, *The Essential Kabbalah*, pp. 83, 84.

context. According to him, reciting the blessing over bread with kav-vanah actually served to spark a reunion between the exiled Shekhi-nah and the formless Godhead.

Two centuries later, a Hasidic teacher, Levi Yitzhak of Berdichev, repeated Luria's teaching almost word for word:

> When you desire to eat or drink, or to fulfill other worldly desires, and you focus your awareness on the love of God, then you elevate that physical desire to spiritual desire. Thereby you draw out the holy spark that dwells within. You bring forth holy sparks from the matcrial world. There is no path greater than this. For wherever you go and whatever you do—even mundane activities—you serve God.[2]

The tendency to split body and mind is so deeply rooted in the human psyche, however, that Levi Yitzhak was compelled to remind his students again and again that the impulse to mortify the the flesh was actually an evil distraction from concentration on the divine emanations embodied in the created world. On the other hand, those who indulge the ego are also in danger. The Hasidic Rabbi Rafael of Bershad presents us with an old folk belief to illustrate the point of going too far to the other side of self-abnegation. "They say that the proud are reborn as bees. For, in his heart, the proud man says: 'I am a writer, I am a singer, I am a great one at studying.' And since what is said of such men is true: that they will not turn to God, not even on the threshold of hell, they are reborn . . . again as bees which hum and buzz: 'I am, I am, I am.' "[3]

The eighteenth-century Italian Kabbalist Moses Chayyim Luz-zatto asserted that the key to avoiding extremes and strengthening one's resolve lay in sanctifying daily life through meditation in action.

2. Matt, *The Essential Kabbalah*, p. 151.
3. Quote in Buber, *Tales of the Hasidim: The Early Masters*, p. 129.

Using the same age-old metaphors, twentieth-century teacher Rabbi Abraham Kook reiterated this central kabbalistic teaching in psychological terms that his contemporaries would readily understand. Outlining the qualities and motivations of spiritual seekers across the spectrum, he divides them into those who look to meditation for personal fulfillment; those whose expanding consciousness includes the entire community of Israel; those whose deepening insight encompasses all humanity; and those who acquire the capacity to embrace all beings in all worlds.

Although Rabbi Kook's language is mystical and poetic, it is clear throughout his writing that practicing Kabbalah is no more esoteric than cultivating the intention to reconcile with the "holy of holies," which is the source of all life. The path consists of performing one's daily activities with kavvanah, the concentrated awareness engendered by a strong commitment to meditation.

Sexuality

Because Jewish guidelines for sexual behavior are considered by many to be outmoded for modern times, twenty-first-century Kabbalists will have to redefine the meaning of unification for themselves. For centuries, the Kabbalah taught that God is both male and female, and—as direct images of the Divine—that human beings are androgynous as well. Abraham Abulafia placed no rules for entry onto the path other than a willing heart and a commitment to the practice. This opened the gates to all kinds of students, regardless of gender or sexual preference, religious beliefs or lack of them. For Abulafia, union was strictly a matter of concentrating on the letters of the Tetragrammaton until all consciousness of self disappeared. Translating mystic oneness in sexual terms thus became a metaphor, used only to guide those who hadn't yet had the experience. It *corresponded* to the sexual act, something they could recognize. But it was to be taken strictly as a metaphor, for no language comprehensible to the dualistic mind could accurately describe the experience of mystic union.

Using the biblical Song of Songs as their source, many Kabbalists extended the sexual metaphor beyond their meditations into their married lives in an effort to enhance their activities. The Baal Shem Tov, for example, experienced the death of his wife as a deeply spiritual loss. When asked by his disciples why he was suffering so badly, he replied, "I was looking forward to rising in a flame. But now [without my wife], I am but half a body, and it is impossible. It is for this reason that I suffer so."[4]

Based on the experience of oneness, of the complete and direct experience of the other as one's self, this kind of male-female relationship makes sense. But to the Baal Shem Tov's disciples, who thought he had no concern for "worldly things," the profound meaning of his wife's death remained an incomprehensible metaphor.

The Baal Shem Tov was also noted for teaching Kabbalah to his talented daughter and bypassing his less gifted son; and although she was permitted to teach in her own right while her father was still alive (from behind a screen, so her male students would not be "distracted" by her beauty), the official mantle of succession went to the male Maggid of Mezerich after the Baal Shem Tov died. (Incidentally, legend has it that even the screen didn't keep men from "falling in love" with the Baal Shem Tov's daughter, because of her beautiful voice.)

Taking the founder's liberalizing impulse a step further, the Hasidic Rabbi Shalom of Belz refused to see women as a distraction and sat with his wife beside him while he taught. As far as Rabbi Shalom was concerned, men and women were "helpmates," their relationship a means of restoring Creation to its original state. No doubt his disciples, too, were puzzled by their teacher's curious behavior.

4. Quoted in Besserman, ed., *The Way of the Jewish Mystics*, pp. 115–116.

Contemporary female Kabbalists are few, but it is through them that the breach between male and female will eventually be repaired. It would be a mistake, as some female teachers are doing, to isolate themselves by creating a strictly women's practice, limiting their instruction by assuming the same narrow-minded legacy of their male forebears. To reject any sincere seeker as a student because of gender, caste, disability, or any other trait would be the opposite of Rabbi Kook's call to compassion. It would be best to follow the example he set at the beginning of the twentieth century when he joined with men and women, devout and secular, Jews and Gentiles, educated and illiterate, and rich and poor to share the fruits of his own hard-won insight.

Food

Kabbalists added their own esoteric interpretation to the Jewish dietary laws. We know, for example, that, depending on their level of spiritual attainment, mystics in the Safed community were given specific instructions regarding food. Under Isaac Luria's leadership, the Cubs ate only two (mostly vegetarian) meals a day, reserving wine and meat for Sabbath and holiday celebrations. Each disciple was assigned a specific set of kavvanot designed to facilitate the proper meditative state of mind at table. Blessings over food were used as occasions to meditate and talking was kept to a minimum as the Cubs sought to release the holy sparks with every bite they took. Since dietary codes and their accompanying meditative techniques were known only to teacher and student, and because the Ari's instructions were designed to suit the capacities and temperaments of specific individuals, we have no records beyond what was known to the Safed community at large. The same holds true for the Hasidic community. There are several homilies about the eating (and fasting) habits of the masters, and a few scattered references showing how some used food as a teaching tool. One anecdote describes how the Baal Shem Tov forbade a student with a particularly bad temper from using a knife when he ate. Another alludes to the first meeting between the Baal Shem Tov and his successor, the Maggid of Mezerich, during which—to the Maggid's dismay— the master spoke of nothing but his coachman's diet. Presumably, there was some very esoteric teaching going on during this exchange, but since we haven't been given the details, we can only guess at the master's intentions.

We are on surer ground when we discuss the food habits of twentieth-century Kabbalists. Rabbi Abraham Kook, for example, was a vegetarian; so, too, was Rabbi Menachem Mendel Schneerson, the last Lubavitcher Rebbe. My own experience with Rabbi Kook's son and successor, Rabbi Zvi Yehudah Kook, disclosed that his father's attitude toward food remained an important part of his spiritual training. Each time I came to sit at Rabbi Zvi Yehudah's table (and every session we spent studying the Lurianic Kabbalah was accompanied by food), I was offered something different to eat. I learned soon enough that not accepting the food the Rabbi was offering to me was tantamount to refusing the teaching. In other words, eating was *itself* the study of Kabbalah. What and when we ate was also essential, I noted. At first I tended to overlook how careful Rabbi Zvi Yehudah was to point out the color, texture, and origin of the food. It struck me as just another eccentricity on the part of this very eccentric teacher. But when I arrived on Tisha b'Av (a day of penance and fasting that commemorates the destruction of the Second Temple in 70 CE) and found the Rabbi seated in front of a big platter of cookies and a tea tray, urging me to partake, I was really shocked. Loath as I was to eat, I bit into a cookie and waited for the explanation I knew would be soon enough in coming. Giving me a merry look, Rabbi Zvi Yehudah began listing the ingredients of the cookies and reciting the names of the bakeries that specialized in producing them. He also had me scrutinize them carefully as he pointed out their shape, color, and texture. As I studied a cookie, he began discoursing on the process by which it had been baked, how the ingredients had been measured and blended. He discussed the origins of every ingredient, going back as far as the seedlings and the earth in which they had been planted. It took a while before it dawned on me that what I was hearing was that day's lesson in Lurianic Kabbalah. In fact, as soon as he'd finished talking and his attendant had cleared away the tea things, the Rabbi dismissed me.

Beyond its simple ethical associations, Rabbi Kook's vegetarianism was directly related to the spiritual level of the practitioner. One who has committed oneself to a life lived in, and as, the source of all life will not kill in order to eat. And because every physical function provides the mystic with an opportunity to bridge the gap between the self and other forms of life, nourishment of body and soul is a simultaneous event. Meditation is therefore an ongoing event in which the sefirot, for example, are no longer symbols but actual, living expressions. Keter, the highest condition available to human consciousness, is embodied in the purest (that is, the least "animalistic") food. Associated with the color white, it would correspond to dairy foods like yogurt, milk, and white cheese. The spiritual level corresponding to Chokhmah, blue, would be found in the non-animal nourishment that comes from the sea, such as agar, seaweed, and salt. Binah, the Mother of life, is represented by all green foods. Gevurah, the red sefirah that is exoterically identified with judgment (and by extension, animal sacrifice) is kabbalistically interpreted as a sacrifice of the ego. In other words, the higher one aims on the Tree of Life, the lower on the food chain one eats. Kabbalists will therefore substitute red foods, such as beets, radishes, cherries, rhubarb, grapes, and watermelon, for meat. The lower sefirot—Tiferet, Netzach, Hod, Yesod, and Malkhut—reflect their higher counterparts.

Similarly, when performed as meditations on the Hebrew letters, the various food blessings serve as reminders of the pervasiveness of the Divine. In this way, every meal becomes a yichud. Permuting the letters of the blessing calls the Kabbalist's attention to the marvelous chemical transformations of the food as it interacts with the body in the digestion process. The Hebrew letters constituting the blessings over the planting, cooking, cleaning, and excreting of food are likewise permuted to focus the mind on the unity of all life.

Purity

Again going beyond the peshat, or literal, interpretation of the Torah, Kabbalists regarded the Jewish purity laws as a hidden set of meditation techniques that would be recognizable only to initiates. Focusing on the injunctions surrounding bodily cleanliness in particular, they used immersion in the *mikvah* (ritual bath) as yet another opportunity for contemplation. Here, in addition to permuting the Hebrew letters of the appropriate mikvah blessings, one would visualize a part of the body and its corresponding sefirah. Putting one's head in the water and permuting the letters of the mikvah blessing, one visualized Keter. Immersing the right arm and reciting the blessing, one visualized Chokhmah; doing the same with the left arm, one visualized Binah; next immersing the right side of the body and reciting the appropriate permutations, one visualized Chesed; repeating the process on the left side, one visualized Gevurah. Immersing the spine, locus of the central nervous system, and permuting the letters corresponding to the structure of the spine, one visualized Tiferet. The procedure continued in similar fashion, with the right leg visualized as Netzach, the left leg as Hod, and the genitals as Yesod. Standing straight up in the water, one completed the meditation by permuting the last part of the blessing and visualizing both feet as Malkhut.

Kabbalah and Mainstream Judaism

The relationship between Kabbalah and mainstream Judaism has not always been comfortable. Considering Kabbalists as "aberrations" in Judaism, antimystical rabbis generally tended to ignore them, a situation that continues today.

The tannaitic mystics of the first century remained acceptable to the religious establishment until the destruction of the Temple in 70 CE. Immediately after that, the biblical meditative practice of the prophets and their tannaitic successors disappeared from mainstream Jewish life. The Kabbalah, as it began to be called, became the property of a self-proclaimed elite—until the thirteenth-century radical Abraham Abulafia challenged this by publicizing the ancient teachings. Prompted by his messianic ambitions, he rebuked his opponents for being less spiritual than the worthy Gentiles among his disciples and declared that they were living the letter rather than the spirit of the Torah. For his outspokenness, Abulafia was rewarded with excommunication.

Abulafia's contemporary, Moses de Leon, chose a more discreet path, circumventing antimystical opinion by legitimizing his teachings as the sacred words of the tannaitic sages themselves. Hidden behind its opaque veil of sefirotic symbolism, the *Zohar* remained inaccessible to the legalists, who—had they detected what he was really up to—would no doubt have excommunicated him, too. Although couched in high-flown mystical language, his denunciation of rabbinic legalism was no less harsh than Abulafia's. He labeled as wicked anyone regarding the Torah as a mere story, and advised the righteous not to be daunted in their desire to look under its outer "garments."

The debate over the "proper" way to read the Torah is as old as the giving of the Torah itself. Secular scholars have quarreled over the authorship, dates, and "revised" versions of the Pentateuch, while religious scholars believe it to be the revealed Word of God written down by Moses. Rationalists see it as the historical, ethical, and political history of the nation called Israel. Rabbinic legal decisors interpret its commandments with the goal of maintaining the moral continuity of social behavior within the Jewish community.

And mystics see it as nothing less than the living embodiment of God. By lending itself to personal experience and individual interpretation, the mystic's view of Torah can become problematic for the greater community. Particularly after the rise of Christianity as an offshoot of Judaism, what might otherwise have been seen as the harmless teaching of a minority of eccentrics became a dangerous heresy. Viewed in this light, one can understand the difficulties encountered by even such an illustrious twentieth-century religious figure as Rabbi Kook, who "taught that all existence is the body of God. . . . secular and holy are not fundamentally distinct; secularism participates in the larger scheme of religious evolution. *Even heresy plays a spiritual role, challenging us to continually expand our concept of God.*"[5]

In 1760, after many tragic events followed the conversion to Islam of pseudo-messiah Sabbatai Zevi, one Rabbi Moses Hagiz informed the Venetian rabbis that another self-proclaimed messiah was living in their midst. Thus began the public hounding of Kabbalist Moses Chayyim Luzzatto, which ended in his flight and excommunication. Only after he had sworn a written oath never again to teach Kabbalah was Luzzatto left to die in peace. The public excommunication of the Maggid of Mezerich and his Hasidim by the rationalist Vilna Gaon is perhaps the best-known example of a rift in Judaism that still exists—albeit to a lesser degree—between rationalists and Hasidim.

5. Quoted in Matt, *The Essential Kabbalah*, p. 16. Emphasis added.

6
Kabbalah and the Supernatural

IN THE MIDDLE AGES, Kabbalah left the confines of its priviliged circle of Jewish initiates and entered the popular realm. Inevitably, the stringent requirements for the teaching and practice of Jewish mysticism were watered down for the masses. By the sixteenth century, the European Neoplatonist philosophers and Christian theologians who had appropriated it were busily altering its symbolism to accommodate their own doctrines. For example, the divine emanations symbolized by the first three sefirot were assigned trinitarian qualities, God's feminine aspect was identified with the Virgin Mary, and God as Beloved became synonymous with Christ. In secular circles, the idea of manipulating nature through the creative power of the Hebrew letters appealed to Renaissance alchemists, astrologers, explorers, and self-styled cosmologists.

Desperate for an end to exile and persecution, the Jewish community itself turned to the Kabbalah as a magical solution. The occultists and false messiahs who proliferated throughout Europe for the next three centuries only served to compound the problem. Superstition and folklore gave literal translation to metaphors that had previously been used as teaching tools for meditation. Mental and physical phenomena arising from meditation were objectified, and

Rabbi Akiva's cautions against taking one's own projections for reality were ignored. Lured into dubious practices by false promises of salvation and immortality, many Jews and Gentiles fancied themselves "Kabbalists." In the typical fashion of occultists, they read the technique of Hebrew letter permutation as a means by which to alter, and even re-create, the physical world of matter. Personifying their own fears and ambitions, they engendered a pantheon of demiurges, spirit guides, demons, and ghosts, which, by the nineteenth century, had become cloaked in the respectable language of "science." Even our own materialistic twentieth century remains witness to a flood of books that purport to explain the mysteries of nature in kabbalistic terms. In fact, so much energy was poured into using the Kabbalah to manipulate nature that its spiritual function all but disappeared. It has taken a generation of Jewish interest in the spiritual traditions of the East to restore it.

Beyond its symbolic visions and esoteric biblical cosmology, what was there about the Kabbalah that lent itself to literal interpretation and made it so attractive to occultists? Two immediate aspects of the practice come to mind: the reincarnation of souls and the spirit guide. The first gave rise to a preoccupation with life after death and, particularly among the uneducated, poverty-stricken inhabitants of the East European ghettos, a belief in demonic possession. No less motivated by fear and the age-old desire for control over the unknown, the second isolated the magician from ordinary members of the community. This phenomenon coincided with the perversion of the idea of the righteous person, the tzaddik, into one who could converse with the spirits of the dead, bring about curses and cures, and call upon angels.

The Golem

Perhaps the most famous Jewish occultist was the nineteenth-century Rabbi Lowy of Prague, creator of the golem, a supposedly superhuman being—which some historians of science claim as the precursor of the modern robot.

According to the legend, Rabbi Lowy, a master of Hebrew letter permutation, shaped a block of inert matter into the form of a man, which he animated by breathing into its nostrils the sacred Names of God. Harmless enough at first, the golem functioned as the rabbi's servant, running errands and doing odd jobs around the house. But further empowered by the master's meditations with the passage of time, the creature began to develop spectacular strength and a will of its own. Rumor had it that the rabbi was attempting to endow the golem with a soul, but that he was having trouble keeping its animal instinct in check and that the creature was going on rampages. Things got so out of hand that the rabbi had to lock the golem in the attic at night. Finally, unable to control it, he had to destroy it. But the legend of the golem continued into the twentieth century, and it still persists. Rabbi Lowy's house in Prague has been turned into a museum, and, in keeping with his instructions, the attic containing the dismantled parts of the golem has never been unlocked. Part of the legend's power is attributed to the strange events surrounding Rabbi Lowy's house during the Nazi invasion of Prague. According to eyewitnesses, the invading soldiers sent in to round up all the city's Jews destroyed every Jewish synagogue and home but Rabbi Lowy's. Adolf Hitler himself had given the order to leave it standing. Having been warned by his astrologers that destroying the house and releasing the golem would lead to his defeat, the maddest occultist of them all deferred to the power of the Kabbalah.

Reincarnation

Gershom Scholem cites the twelfth-century *Sefer Bahir* as the first kabbalistic reference to the idea that the soul travels from one body to another after physical death. Identifying Jewish mysticism as an antiphilosophical, anti-Aristotelian phenomenon and likening it to its Christian and Islamic counterparts, he links the three dualistic (and therefore heretical) traditions under the common heading of "Gnosticism." Defining the kabbalistic term *gilgul* as, "literally, 'turning over' or 'rolling over,' "[1] he asserts that the underlying assumption in all three dualistic belief systems is the desire for redemption outside of the physical body. Impeccable as his scholarship is, however, Scholem's literal interpretation of the term distracts him from its symbolic function. To the practitioner of Kabbalah, the soul is neither a physical nor an ethereal entity, but a figurative representation of a level of human consciousness. Whether it is referred to as ruach, neshamah, or nefesh, the soul corresponds to a stage in the meditation process. Therefore, rather than transmigrating, literally, from body to body after death, the soul (consciousness) "rolls" and "skips" from one world (sefirah) to the next as it "ascends" in meditation to the highest realm of nonthought.

In their instruction manuals, mystics from the Merkavah period to the present point out that the ruach level of the soul is synonymous with the breath, and that "planting" alludes to a meditative technique which demands a lifelong commitment to the practice of permuting and chanting the sacred Names. In this context, instead of reading the following passages quoted by Scholem from the *Bahir* as a rationale for the idea of reincarnation, it would be more helpful to see them as a disguised set of meditation instructions.

> "He ceased from work and rested" [Exodus 31:17]. . . . This teaches that from thence all the souls fly out, as is said, "He ceased from work [*shavat*; which can be read as *shabbat*, 'Sabbath'] and rested." To a thousand generations, as is said: "The word which He commanded to a thousand generations" [Psalms 105:8].

1. Gershom Scholem. *On the Mystical Shape of the Godhead* (New York: Schocken Books, 1991), p. 201.

. . . Go and see. This is like a person who has planted a vineyard in his garden, and he hoped it should bring forth wild grapes, and it brought forth wild grapes [after Isaiah 5:2]. He saw that he was not succeeding—so he replanted it, placed a fence around it, repaired the breaches, pruned [the vines of] the wild grapes, and planted it a second time. He saw that he was not succeeding—he again fenced it off, and again replanted it after pruning it. How often? He said to them: Until a thousand generations, as is written: "He commanded a word to a thousand generations" [Psalms 105:8]. This is what is meant by the [talmudic] saying [*Hagigah* 13b]: "Nine hundred seventy-four generations were lacking [for the figure of one thousand], when the Holy One, blessed be He, stood and planted them in every generation."[2]

In the first passage, the "rest" that follows the image of the souls flying out corresponds to the period assigned to holding the exhalation while permuting the letters of the sacred Name a thousand times. The second passage gives preparatory instructions for the meditation technique known as planting. One is enjoined to "place a fence" around the area (isolate oneself from worldly affairs in meditation, hitbodedut); to engage in "repairing" the breaches around the grapevines (perform a tikkun meditation linking one's consciousness to one of the red or green lower or upper sefirot); and to "prune" distracting thoughts before reciting the Names no less than a thousand times.

Where Scholem goes on to argue that the *Bahir*'s references to "garments" stand for the numerous impure physical bodies assumed by the human soul in transmigration (including those of animals!), we ought to see these as prefiguring the *Zohar*, which warns aspirants not to be fooled by the "garments" (i.e., the exoteric level of the Torah) that hide the Shekhinah from the uninitiated.

2. Scholem, *On the Mystical Shape of the Godhead*, p. 201.

Filtered through the limited understanding of the masses, such literal readings of kabbalistic texts reinforced popular notions about sin and punishment and merit and reward. Originally reserved for sinners alone, the concept of reincarnation was expanded in the thirteenth and fourteenth centuries to include the souls of the patriarchs and matriarchs, as well as the righteous and the childless. This tendency to toss everything into the pot and call it Kabbalah marks the point where speculation about Jewish mystical texts began to compel more interest than the practice itself.

The idea that one soul could acquire traits or qualities embedded in the "sparks" of other souls (which can be traced to the Safed mystics' practice of seeking inspiration from great past masters by meditating on or near their gravesites) also mistakes a meditative procedure for a magical rite. We know that, based on their temperaments and levels of spiritual development, Luria's disciples were assigned specific sefirot for meditation. And since the righteous were viewed as spiritual vehicles for the linking of consciousness with the sefirot, taking sparks from the souls of the righteous does not mean, literally, merging with other souls during the transmigration process, but rather directing one's meditation to the spiritual quality inherent in one's assigned sefirah while one is still alive. The crude folklore that emerged from the popularization of kabbalistic practices is responsible not only for the notion that one's soul can be empowered by the righteous, but for the pervasive nineteenth-century belief that evil or demonic sparks may also accompany the soul's journey. Worse yet, a misguided soul might even land in the body of an animal. And, according to the legend of the *dybbuk*, a wretched or vengeful soul could cannibalize its victims by occupying the body of a living host. To counter such demonic possession, ignorant village healers and self-styled masters of gematria improvised nonsense formulas and excorcisms in a hodgepodge gleaned from purportedly ancient kabbalistic texts.

Attributing responsibility to books like the *Bahir* and the *Zohar* for such distortions is fruitless. But perpetuating the idea that Kabbalah is synonymous with occultism or that Kabbalists were magicians with great supernatural powers is to devalue the legitimacy of Jewish spiritual practice. Equating high spiritual development with the ability to read the future from the lines of faces and palms, or determining which parts of one's soul needs to be "perfected" by transmigrating through a variety of out-of- body experiences in otherworldly realms is to debase the efforts of seriously committed Kabbalists. That the image of Adam Kadmon was recast to meet superstitious notions about reincarnation is one sad, but vivid, example of how the Kabbalah was transformed from a spiritual discipline into an occult system.

Originally regarded as a stage of visualization in which one meets oneself in the form of the androgynous Adam, the figure of the cosmic man on the Throne was taken by medieval occultists to be a literal manifestation of Adam as he appears in Genesis. Inverting the metaphor of Adam Kadmon, they attributed all forms of human wickedness to the "Ungodly Adam." Where the Merkavah mystic would permute and chant the letters that constituted the limbs of the cosmic body of Adam Kadmon, readers of *Tikkunei Zohar*, an anonymous medieval text, interpreted the letters and numbers of the Names as an opportunity to erase Adam's sin by elevating the sparks from each individual limb of one's own physical body in the act of transmigration. This literal reading of a mandala, once used for developing deeper levels of concentration through chanting and visualization, now gave rise to such far-fetched conclusions as: barrenness in a woman is the result of a man's soul incarnating in a woman's body, and vice versa; Adam's original sins are still being reincarnated through his children; a soul can be "impregnated" by another soul; souls can group together in "families"; and Jewish souls in particular never reincarnate in animal bodies. One wonders at this point what such conjectures have to do with the mystic's aim of losing the self in No-thingness.

By the sixteenth century, the inverted image of the cosmic man on the heavenly Throne became synonymous with exile. After Isaac Luria's death, his successors fell to speculating about the conceptual meaning of his teaching, and a new version of the Kabbalah was born. In this rationale for political exile and suffering, it was said that branches of the sefirotic Tree had separated from its trunk and roots in a process called *tzimtzum* (contraction). God's light had been too brilliant for the material vessels into which it had emanated, and they shattered. The divine sparks emerging from the broken vessels had blended with the souls of all created things, bringing along with them the *kelippot*, husks of matter, that were ultimately responsible for the evil that escaped into the Creation. It was the duty of the individual Kabbalist to purify his or her own soul of the evil husks clinging to it through endless rounds of transmigration, and, by connecting the soul to its root on the sefirotic Tree, to repair the shattered vessels and return all Creation to its Source. Thus construed, the metaphors that Luria had used to guide his students in meditation (yichud) were turned into a case for reincarnation. No wonder, then, that a literal reading of Cain as the "left shoulder" of Adam (Gevurah) should result in Chayyim Vital's puzzling assertion that Cain was a prophet who "will be infinitely higher than Abel [Chesed]."[3] But when read from the meditator's perspective, there is nothing odd about the statement. Assuming that Vital is referring to the sefirot at the level of the Small Face of the cosmic man, Gevurah (Cain) in the archetypal world of Yetzirah represents a higher stage of meditation than Chesed (Abel) in the archetypal world of Assiah.

Another kabbalistic practice that was changed to conform to ideas about reincarnation was Vital's injunction to merge with the Torah instead of studying it. When he warns his disciples that they will have to "transmigrate" until they fulfill their goal of becoming one

3. Scholem, *On the Mystical Shape of the Godhead*, p. 236.

with the Torah (Shekhinah), he is not speaking of physical reincarnation but of the continued meditative effort required in ascending the cosmic Tree.

Spirit Guides

Problematic because of its dualistic implications, the concept of the *tzelem*, double or spirit guide, nonetheless appears throughout the kabbalistic teachings. Variously interpreted as an astral body, a psychological projection, and a manifestation of the Shekhinah, the tzelem is emblematic of a highly concentrated stage in the meditation process. Abulafia outlined the possibilities inherent in this condition of awareness and urged his followers to exert great caution when engaging in it. He referred to this level of meditation as the dwelling place of spirits, or the third rung of the ladder, a phase where the student's breath was so deep and slow as to be almost imperceptible. Paralleling the Merkavah mystic's experience of meeting himself in ethereal form, the experience opened possibilities for self-understanding that the aspirant hadn't encountered before. And unless one was careful, the projected image of oneself could become harmful. In an instant, angelic beings perceived as helpers and guides could be transformed into *shedim*, demonic obstructors. One could infuse oneself with the power symbolized by such mental forms in a binding exercise, but such meditations were not for the weak-minded. The danger of following one's mental projections and going insane was made clear by the tannaitic sages; and they always meditated in groups to forestall such possibilities. But, as we have seen in the case of Rabbi Akiva's companions, even the greatest masters could fall prey to the hallucinations that accompany alterations in breathing patterns and result in sensory disorientation. Unless one is genuinely meditating for the sake of experiencing the No-thingness of the self, and not for the purpose of acquiring supernatural power, there is always the possibility of self-deception. Yet, as clear-headed teachers and committed disciples were outpaced by growing numbers of occultists and their mass followings, belief in astral projection and the "materialization" of spirit guides grew more pervasive.

The double, or exact likeness seen during the sense-disorienting letter permutations performed by Abulafian Kabbalists, was transformed into the idea that this higher, purer version of the human self (what Greek Neoplatonists called a person's "daemon") was actually an angel, a guardian that was always on call to perform its master's bidding. All one had to do to get one's angel to predict and influence the course of the future was to work oneself into an ecstatic state.

Abulafia's own prophecies no doubt fueled aspirants with the desire to become prophets themselves. By all accounts, most of his immediate disciples were willing to undergo the purification and training required to perfect their natures. But those who followed the Abulafian path after his death were more inclined to evoke spirit guides for less spiritual ends. Communication with celestial beings became the rage in kabbalistic circles from the sixteenth through eighteenth centuries. Jacob of Marvege, a Provençal Kabbalist, even collected a whole manual of "questions for heavenly messengers," and Rabbi Joseph Taytazak made evocation of spirit guides a group practice.

However, the angelic maggid who appeared at Joseph Caro's Friday-night table in sixteenth-century Safed to guide him through the secret mysteries of the Torah had little attraction for eighteenth-century Christian Kabbalists, such as the anonymous author of *The Book of the Secret Magic of Abra-Melin the Mage, as delivered by Abraham the Jew unto His Son Lamech*. In the nineteenth century, particularly in England and France, such pseudo-kabbalistic texts became authoritative sources, replacing the Jewish Kabbalah with a theosophical version that is still widely circulated today. The simultaneous growth of interest in a whole variety of supernatural phenomena—such as spiritualism, phrenology, hypnotism, magnetism, and the survival of the body after physical death—saw the angelic guardian transformed into the human astral body. Materialists in the new industrial age, who aspired less to egolessness than to making fortunes, manipulated what was left of the teachings for their own utilitarian ends. By the twentieth century, Kabbalah and supernaturalism had become indistinguishable.

7

Instructions for Beginning Meditation

Yesod / Foundation

RABBI ARYEH KAPLAN's groundbreaking translations of kabbalistic meditation manuscripts not only revived a moribund spiritual tradition, they opened it to contemporary seekers who were unaware that a "Jewish practice" existed at all. Before that, most Kabbalah scholars had focused solely on its historical, cultural, and religious aspects, making no attempt to decode its impenetrable meditative techniques. It took Rabbi Kaplan's course on Jewish meditation to spark worldwide interest in applying the ancient wisdom of the Kabbalah to life in the real world of today. Adding traditional kabbalistic meditation exercises and intensive study of Eastern techniques to his years of dedicated Torah scholarship, he came up with something entirely new and original for the practice of spirituality in a Jewish context. Kaplan's own teaching was cut off by his tragic death at age forty-eight, but the powerful spiritual engine he set into motion is still charging along at a lively pace. The following instructions for beginning meditation are offered in tribute to him.

Assiah / Action

Reading, study, and quiet introspection form the threshold of pardes, the four-leveled garden of Kabbalah. Informing oneself on the subject before beginning is a vital part of the practice and ought not be dispensed with, no matter how eager one is to meditate. (A suggested list of titles is provided at the end of this book.) On completing this preparatory phase, the seeker enters the gate to encounter peshat, the first level of practice, representing the cultivation of a strong rational mind and a healthy ego. It is particularly important at this stage to heed the parable of Rabbi Akiva and his associates, for it gives the "caution" sign to mentally agitated people who might otherwise rush into meditation hoping to acquire supernatural powers, as well as to those seeking a cure-all for physical and psychological problems.

The second stage of practice, remez, entails the commitment to living a righteous life. Here, rather than merely *studying* the Torah, the seeker *becomes* the Torah by expressing the commandments in one's daily activity.

The third stage, derash, represents the creative, devotional aspect of the practice. It is the "juice" fuelling the seeker's desire to "meet the Beloved"; it is the way of the heart that keeps regular meditation from becoming a rote intellectual exercise.

The fourth stage, sod, entails the willingness to seclude oneself in daily meditation (hitbodedut) and, like Rabbi Akiva, to integrate the fruits of one's meditation as an ordinary person in this world of "coming and going."

As with all spiritual traditions, the Kabbalah should be undertaken with a qualified teacher and is best practiced with a like-minded group. Locating the right community of mystical companions is the responsibility of the seeker. Aspiring Kabbalists must search around, attend workshops, study groups, and seminars, and make inquiries until they find a community suited to their individual needs and temperaments.

Yetzirah / Formation

In the following instructions, all breathing exercises should be performed by inhaling and exhaling through the nose, not the mouth. No attempt should be made to force or change the natural flow of your breath. Avoid meditations that require you to hold your breath for any length of time if you suffer from respiratory, heart, or blood-pressure problems, dizziness, or neurological illness. If you are taking medication, check with your physician before embarking on any course of meditation.

GAZING

Described in chapter 2, this traditional meditation on Chesed has been slightly modified to broaden the concept of mercy to include lovingkindness for all beings.

Sit on a chair with no armrests, your feet firmly planted on the floor, or sit on a floor cushion with legs crossed and your head, neck, and spine held straight. Breathing quietly, look down at your hand. When your mind is quiet, let yourself begin breathing the word *Chesed*, mercy, allowing the inhalation to form the first syllable, *Che*, and the exhalation to form the last syllable, *sed*. Continue for twenty-five minutes, returning attention to the hand and breath if your mind wanders. When finished, take a few breaths, stretch and rotate your head gently before getting up.

LISTENING

Adapted from the teaching of the Maggid of Mezerich, this Hasidic technique focuses on the sounds of the world to bring the meditator to the experience of "no-sound," a condition for dissolving the self in No-thingness.

Seated in an upright position on the floor or on a chair, eyes partly closed and breathing easily, concentrate all your attention on the sounds coming in through your ears. Let your concentration deepen until you feel that your entire body is one great ear absorbing the sounds. Don't allow your mind to comment on what is coming in. If your mind starts making associations to the sounds or wandering in any way, stop and draw your attention back to the sound of your breath. When the mind has quieted, return once again to concentrating on the sounds. Do this for twenty-five minutes. Then take a few breaths, stretch, and rotate your head gently before getting up.

SWALLOWING

Combining visualization and sound, Isaac Luria designed this unique method for permuting the sacred Name (YHVH). It is presented here using the sefirah Chesed (Mercy), its corresponding color (white), and Name (El), and the right arm.

Seated in a meditation posture on a chair or on a floor cushion, relax into regular breathing. When your mind and body are still, visualize your right arm as the white sefirah Chesed. Holding your breath and moving only your larynx and tongue, repeat the word *El* ten times. Then take another breath and resume your repetition of the Name. Continue visualizing and reciting thus for twenty-five minutes. (Do not strain to hold your breath. If you cannot do so for ten recitations, then try it in sets of five.) When finished, take a few breaths, rotate your head, and be sure you are steady on your feet before standing.

BINDING

The intention of this yichud is to harmonize the polarities within the body and the mind. The old teachers customized their instructions to accommodate the degree of spiritual accomplishment of each student. This general version is intended to reconcile the "male" and "female" elements residing in all human beings, regardless of their meditation experience, gender, or sexual preference.

Seated in a meditation posture on a chair or floor cushion with eyes closed, visualize your own body as the cosmic Tree of Life. The left side is female, represented as the red sefirah Gevurah (Judgment); the right side is male, represented as the white sefirah Chesed. When your breath and mind are calm and your concentration on the sefirot is firmly established, you may begin to "bind" the two by visualizing them merging at the heart center. Here, concentrate your attention on the merged sefirot as the harmonious, undifferentiated form of Tiferet (Beauty), white blending into red and vice versa, until no color exists at all. The binding meditation should be performed for twenty-five minutes. When finished, slowly open your eyes and take a few breaths before getting up. Rest your eyes if any afterimages remain.

CLIMBING

Taken from the Merkavah mystics, this meditation is designed to bring the practitioner to the experience of Ein, No-thing. Because it combines visualization and some degree of letter permutation, it might prove difficult for beginners and should be undertaken only after performing each of those separately at first.

In a seated meditation posture, visualize yourself climbing Mount Sinai. Engaging all your senses, feel the sun's warmth, smell the air, hear the sound of the wind, and so on. On reaching the summit, gaze into the empty sky. When the sky has merged with the horizon line to produce a void, visualize a circle within the void that contains the black letters *Yod, Heh, Vav, Heh* on white parchment. Once the image is clear, visualize the circle spinning until the black letters merge with the white parchment background. See the circle spin until the letters blur and finally disappear, leaving nothing but the void. Continue breathing and meditating on the void until twenty-five minutes have elapsed. Make sure your breath is relaxed and your eyes are focused before standing.

BUILDING

The Maggid of Mezerich devised this preliminary meditation to help his students eliminate distracting thoughts. Corresponding to God's seven days of creating ("building") the universe are the seven lower sefirot—Chesed, Gevurah, Tiferet, Netzach, Hod, Yesod, and Malkhut—representing the edifice of human consciousness. Working in stages, the practitioner strengthens concentration by (1) locating the appropriate sefirotic source of each thought, (2) isolating it, and (3) "building" it into a strength. For example, if a selfish or lustful thought is experienced as a distraction, one may locate its source in Tiferet or Malkhut. By bringing the thought to Chesed, one transforms selfishness or lust into mercy or lovingkindness.

In the case of more stubborn thoughts, the Maggid advised breaking them down letter by letter until they made no sense at all.

Having memorized the sefirot and their corresponding qualities, sit in a meditation posture on a chair or floor cushion. When your breathing is regular and you are relaxed, let the thoughts pass through your mind, neither clinging to them nor trying to avoid them. If you find yourself focusing on one particular bothersome thought, label it. Say, for example, you are distracted by resentment against some person or life situation. After locating your resentment on the left side of the tree in the red sefirah of Gevurah, visualize it moving up to the green sefirah of Binah on the left side and being transformed into Understanding.

If your "building" is weak and the thought recurs, deconstruct the word *resentment* by breaking it down into its individual letter components, one by one. Visualize the letters disintegrating and returning to their source in "no-thought."

When your resentment has disappeared, center your mind on

your breath without labeling your thoughts. The meditation should last no more than twenty-five minutes.

TIMING

Creating a daily meditation schedule and keeping to it is probably the most important aspect of any spiritual practice. The three periods of Jewish daily prayer enabled Safed Kabbalists to use the liturgy as an occasion for group meditation. For this purpose, Isaac Luria assigned each sefirah its own time of day, corresponding color, trait, sacred Name, and symbolic biblical figure. Here is Luria's meditation on Chesed.

Rising at dawn, seat yourself in a meditation posture and visualize the white sefirah Chesed, seeing the the Name El at the center. When you have firmly established the image, visualize yourself entering the sefirah as the figure of Abraham, merging and becoming one with Lovingkindness. Breathing regularly, allow the the images to dissolve into the sefirah, hearing only the sound of your breath emerging as the sound El. Continue the imageless meditation until twenty-five minutes have elapsed. As always, take a few breaths and allow your eyes to grow accustomed to the light and the objects in the room before getting up.

SANCTIFYING

A variation on the above Lurianic meditation, the following visualization is designed to help you in preparing any activity of importance (e.g., making a life change such as career, marriage, divorce, move, or having a child) that you wish to sanctify.

Seated in a meditation posture and establishing a regular breathing pattern, visualize the sefirot Chokhmah (Wisdom) and Binah (Understanding) as a circle and a square, respectively. Let the thought of your intended activity dissolve into the two sefirot, seeing the circle and square drawing near to each other and finally merging. Articulate the thought of your impending activity only once, at the outset of the meditation. Spend the remainder of the twenty-five-minute meditation period concentrating your attention on the sefirot.

Atzilut / Emanation

COSMIC DANCING

Moses de Leon often cast his instructions in the form of intricately textured prose and poetry. The following is a simplified version of a *Zohar* meditation focusing on the highest sefirot in the world of Atzilut, Emanation. The technique is intended to heighten one's power of concentration. It can be especially helpful in quieting a busy mind.

Sit in a meditation posture on a chair or floor cushion with eyes closed. Breathing regularly, visualize the cosmic Tree of Life, each sefirah emanating its own ray of color:

Keter	white/black
Chokhmah	blue
Binah	green
Gevurah	red
Chesed	white

Once the sefirot are firmly captured in your mind's eye, you may begin to "move" them about, seeing the colored rays engaging in a cosmic dance. For example, Keter radiates down to Chokhmah, which joins its blue ray to the green of Binah, and so on. See the colored rays merging, moving downward, reversing direction and moving upward, and crossing left and right in constant motion. Then, gradually slowing them down, bring each colored ray back to its original place on the sefirotic Tree. If you grow tired or feel any strain, return to visualizing the sefirotic colors in their static position on the tree. Continue until twenty-five minutes have elapsed. Before getting up, be sure to blink your eyes a few times and accustom yourself to the light and the shapes in the room.

THE STILL, SMALL VOICE

This Hasidic technique, devised by Rabbi Nachman of Breslov, imparts a personal note to Isaac Luria's swallowing meditation. The great-grandson of the Baal Shem Tov, Nachman was known as an extremely sensitive teacher who emphasized emotion over intellect. His meditations are therefore particularly recommended for "left-brain" people who need to enhance the devotional side of their practice.

Sitting in a meditation posture on a chair or floor cushion alone in your room, establish a calm and steady breathing pattern before beginning to "hear" the sound of your voice emerging as a mental "scream." As the scream grows clearer, hear it form the phrase *Ribbono shel olam* (Master of the universe). Allow the sound of the scream to grow more urgent until you are literally *breathing* it. Once you have firmly established your concentration, draw the breath/scream from your lungs to your lips, feeling it move through your nasal passages to the nerve centers in your brain. As the scream travels through your nerves, it may produce a faint sound by activating the vocal cords. Continue meditating this way for twenty-five minutes.

The "still, small voice" meditation may also be performed without using words. This form is particularly recommended if one wishes to recall oneself to the practice at small intervals while engaged in daily activities.

MEDITATION ON INCENSE

The *Zohar*'s interpretation of the burning of incense in the Temple is the basis for a meditation on sacrificing negative emotions. When regarded as an "offering" or "sacrifice" of the ego, it is particularly useful in reducing anger.

Seated in a meditation posture on a chair or floor cushion before a table, place a stick of incense in a holder and light it. The scent of the incense should not be too sweet or overpowering. Use a short stick that will burn no longer than twenty-five minutes. (Those who are allergic to incense smoke may visualize themselves preparing and lighting the incense rather than actually doing it.) Sit in front of the incense as close or as far away as is comfortable for you and, with eyes closed, breathe rhythmically, inhaling and exhaling the aroma while visualizing the "fire" of your emotions dissolving as the smoke. Do *not* force your breath or attempt to *actually* breathe in the smoke of the incense. The purpose of the meditation is not to become one with the smoke, but rather to dissolve one's negative emotions in it. Perform for twenty-five minutes. Before leaving the room, make sure that the incense has burned all the way down and that no sparks remain.

GERUSHIN (CONTEMPLATION)

Because the Torah is the living embodiment of formless reality, generations of Kabbalists have focused their meditations on its contents; any aspect of it can serve to bring the aspirant to an experience of God. A brilliant Torah scholar, Isaac Luria was noted for making biblical verse and traditional liturgy an essential part of his teaching. The following represents several of his contemplative techniques condensed into one. (A reading knowledge of Hebrew is required.)

Seated in a meditation posture on a chair or floor cushion and holding a Hebrew version of the Bible, open it to any page. (If you have a favorite passage, you may turn to it.) After stilling your mind and relaxing into your breath, begin contemplating the passage you have selected. Once your kavvanah is established and you are fully absorbed—that is, not *thinking* about its meaning—close your eyes and visualize the black letters of the passage and the white spaces between them. Next, visualize the letters and spaces changing places and reversing colors. Keep watching until both letters and spaces entirely disappear. When this has happened, continue contemplating the empty space. At the end of twenty-five minutes, open your eyes and return your attention to the passage as it appears in the Bible. Take a few breaths, blink your eyes, and rotate your head before closing the book and getting up.

SHEFA (DIVINE INFLUX)

As pointed out throughout this book, the dissolution of the self in No-thingness is the primary aim of Jewish meditation. Kabbalists have described the experience in ecstatic terms, some likening it to being bathed in divine light. The "descent" of the shefa indicates a profound condition of meditative absorption.

Seat yourself in a quiet room, as insulated as possible from outside sounds and sights. The best time to do this is after midnight. Close your eyes and ease your mind of thoughts. Breathing regularly, feel your body growing lighter, until you no longer sense yourself as having a body at all. Focus your attention on the sefirah Chokhmah, Wisdom, as your spiritual essence, the root of your being. Visualize your spiritual essence occupying the center of the sefirah and transmitting Wisdom throughout the universe as light. When twenty-five minutes have elapsed, take a few breaths, blink your eyes, and rotate your head before rising.

SHEMA (HEAR O ISRAEL)

A variation on the ancient chanting of the sacred Name once performed by the Temple priests, daily meditation on the Shema is the mainstay of kabbalistic prayer. The version offered here combines elements introduced by Moses de Leon, Abraham Abulafia, Isaac Luria, and the Baal Shem Tov. Appearing twice daily in the prayer service, the six-word phrase—*Shema Yisrael Adonai Eloheinu Adonai Echad*—is actually a yichud that condenses six meditations into one, each symbolizing the six directions and their unification in the One Name. The first word, *Shema* (Hear), also contains the word *shem* (name). The second word, *Yisrael* (Israel), stands for the sefirah Tiferet and the patriarch Jacob. Its Hebrew characters can be separated into two syllables (*yashar-El*), permuting the word Israel into the phrase "straight to God." Since the community of Israel is identified with the female sefirah Malkhut, and the Beloved with the male sefirah Tiferet, recitation of the Shema harmonizes immanence and transcendence.

The remaining four words of the phrase—*Adonai* (YHVH), *Eloheinu* (our God), *Adonai* (YHVH), *Echad* (One)—state that all aspects of God are One. This mystery of faith affirms the completeness of the Name and its attributes. YHVH and all its manifestations are one; Creator and Creation are one; oral and written Torah are one; meditator and object of meditation are one; and "higher" and "lower" worlds symbolically unite as the recitation is sung and the mind avows the unity of the sefirot.

Seated in a meditation posture on a chair or floor cushion, your breathing relaxed and your eyes closed, mentally recite the phrase *Shema Yisrael Adonai Eloheinu Adonai Echad*. When you have cleared the mind of everything but the Shema, you may begin matching its individual words to your breath, using one breath (i.e., one complete inhalation and exhalation) to articulate each word. Next, concentrate your attention on the word *Echad* (One), dwelling on it twice as long as the rest of the words in the phrase. This means drawing out the length of each syllable (*Eh-chad*) and emphasizing the last letter, *d* (Dalet, the fourth letter of the Hebrew alphabet), which is synonymous with the sefirah Gevurah. You may amplify your recitation by visualizing this red sefirah. (The *Zohar* cites Rabbi Shimon bar Yochai to remind us that dwelling on the sefirah of Judgment while reciting the Shema reveals our "insignificance" and thereby helps loosen the ego's hold on us.)

Continue concentrating on *Eh-chad* until your breath and the sound have merged and you are no longer consciously articulating the word but "breathing" it. Continue for twenty-five minutes, after which you may wish to complete the recitation with the following phrase: *Baruch shem kevod malkhuto le-olam va-ed* (Blessed be the Name of the glory of His kingdom forever and ever). This completes the binding of the many and the One, and the unification of mind, body, and breath brought about by the meditation. Perform for twenty-five minutes. Then, take a few breaths, rotate your head, and open your eyes and adjust them to the light and shapes in the room before getting up.

Beriah / Creation

TZERUF (PERMUTATION)

Abraham Abulafia's ecstatic letter meditations often brought mixed results. Many were unprepared for the negative physical effects resulting from the sleeplessness, fasting, and lengthy hours of permutation that he demanded of his students. Judging Abulafia's short path to illumination to be too strenuous, most later Kabbalists eliminated it from their teaching. Though simplified and abbreviated, the tzeruf meditation presented here nonetheless remains true to its source.

Seated in a meditation posture on a chair or floor cushion, follow your breath until it falls into a regular pattern. Make sure you are relaxed and not forcing your breathing. Form your lips in the shape of an oval, but do not open your mouth. You may now begin coordinating your breath with the pronunciation of the Tetragrammaton. Inhale, and then exhale as the sound *Yah*. Inhale again, and exhale as the sound *veh*. Continue breathing this way, using each sound until twenty-five minutes have elapsed. Take a few minutes to adjust your breath and your body condition before standing up.

HAGAH (CHANTING)

Meditation on the Hebrew letters assumed many forms. Kabbalists favored none more than those designed to be chanted, sung, or danced. This one involves turning one's own body into an expression of the sacred Name.

With eyes partly open, but not focusing on any point, and standing with feet together—head, neck, and shoulders held straight—breathe the sound *Yahveh* (YHVH) by inhaling the first syllable and exhaling the second (*Yah-veh*). Once you have established a comfortable rhythm, articulate the syllables out loud, bowing from the waist while chanting *Yah* and holding the bow for as long as it takes to draw out the sound. Rise to your original straight-backed position on completing the chant with the syllable *veh*.

Once you have familiarized yourself with the meditation, you may visualize your spinal column "folding" and "unfolding" in a gesture symbolizing the "bowing" of your ego to its original condition in Nothingness. Perform for twenty-five minutes before rotating your head and adjusting your eyes to the light and objects in the room.

CHAKIKAH (ENGRAVING)

Like all Abraham Abulafia's teachings, the engraving meditation presented here has been recast and simplified for beginners. However, it is important to understand that by engaging the optic nerve, any visualization, even the least strenuous, can cause sensory disorientation. (Anyone who has gazed even briefly at a painting by the Op artist Victor Vasarely has experienced this.) Since sensory disorientation is not the goal of Hebrew letter visualization, it would be a good idea to perform the Abulafian meditations in the company of at least one other person to help you stay grounded.

Sitting in a meditation posture and relaxing into even breathing, with your eyes partly open, visualize the Hebrew letters of the Tetragrammaton (YHVH) until they start to move. As you watch them interweaving, growing, diminishing, changing positions, allow yourself to disappear into the letters. Maintain total concentration on the letters. If you are distracted by any thought, take a few breaths, blink your eyes, and discontinue the meditation. Otherwise, chakikah may be performed for the entire twenty-five-minute period.

CHATZIVAH (HEWING)

A simple Abulafian meditation combining breath and letter visualization, hewing is used to clear the mind of extraneous thoughts while at the same time deepening concentration. The fact that it is not as complex as the other Hebrew letter meditations offered above only belies its potency. In meditation, the simplest exercises are most often the hardest to sustain. Because they seem to demand so little of one's attention, the mind can become flooded with thoughts. On the other hand, when all of one's awareness is gathered and stored in one small spot, the concentrated energy produced is enormous.

Seated in a meditative posture, spend the first five minutes concentrating on the flow of your breath. When a rhythmic pattern of breathing has been established, begin visualizing the Hebrew letters of the Tetragrammaton (see Figure 1 on page 11) so that the rhythm of your breath matches the appearance of each letter. Allow one inhalation and exhalation per letter. If the letters "move" with the breath, let them, but do not try to force it. Breathe and visualize in this way for twenty-five minutes. Don't forget to adjust your eyes to the light and objects in the room and rotate your head before getting up.

8
Kabbalah for the
Twenty-first Century

Twenty years ago, I wrote in the epilogue to my book *Kabbalah: The Way of the Jewish Mystic*, [1] "Today there are no actively recruiting Kabbalists—no posters on college campuses announcing intensive meditation sessions, no encounters, only every now and then a scholarly Kabbalist who might drop a hint or two in a lecture on Jewish mysticism." Now, as we approach the end of the century, it appears that Jewish mysticism is enjoying a renewal. Thanks to a scholarly revival, lucid translations of the ancient texts have made the practice accessible to a new generation of students, and, following in the footsteps of mystics like Abraham Abulafia, Israel Baal Shem Tov, and Abraham Kook, liberal teachers have opened their doors to all sincere seekers. By way of Eastern disciplines such as Yoga and Zen, the Kabbalah has resumed its original emphasis on meditation practice; and a strong feminist influence has added a whole new dimension to Jewish spirituality. The future looks promising. Yet in light of recent cultural, political, and scientific developments on our "small planet," one can't help but wonder whether

1. See under Perle Epstein in the suggested readings section.

there will be a place in the twenty-first century for mysticism of any kind.

Will the desire to become immortal through cloning overcome the longing to lose the self in No-thingness? Will communicating via the Internet with one's teacher and mystical companions ever be able to approximate the experience of the Cubs of Safed or the Merkavah mystics of the Greater and Lesser Assembly? How should the Jewish laws pertaining to work, nature, sexuality, family life, aging, and death be reinterpreted, when ethical issues surrounding marriage, childbearing, abortion, organ transplants, animal rights, the environment, and the right to die are being redefined almost daily? With its mystical emphasis on simplicity and selflessness, will the Kabbalah be able to survive in a world of dizzying technological leaps and increasing acquisitiveness?

Not being a prophet, I have no answers for these questions. Nonetheless, I would like to offer some suggestions on how the Kabbalah might be incorporated into the lives of spiritual seekers in the next century.

Secularism

For centuries, Jewish mysticism was practiced by observant Jews. Masters and students of Kabbalah were conversant with the Jewish laws and considered themselves members of the Orthodox Jewish community. Until Abraham Abulafia invited non-Jews to become his students, there was no such thing as a "secular" Kabbalah; and even among his fellow mystics, Abulafia remained an aberration. Abulafia's secularizing impulse was further set back by false messiahs like Sabbatai Zevi and Joseph Frank. In spite of its radical reputation, Hasidism too is steeped in Orthodox Judaism. There may be disagreements between mystics and Mitnagdim (rationalists) on scholarly interpretations of the Torah and styles of prayer, but members of both groups adhere vigorously to the same Orthodox interpretation of the Jewish laws. You will find no Hasid eating unkosher food or driving a car on the Sabbath. It's even hard to tell the Hasidim and the Mitnagdim apart from the way they dress. The men in both groups wear the same black hats and coats and let the fringes of their *tallit katan* (small prayer shawl worn under the clothing) show over their trousers; and the women wear the same head coverings, long-sleeved blouses, and long skirts. Is there, then, such a thing as a "secular Kabbalist," or are the terms mutually exclusive?

The first twentieth-century teacher to make an attempt at bridging the gap between secular and orthodox spiritual seekers was Rabbi Abraham Kook. Embracing observant and nonobservant Jews alike, he spread his message of mystical Zionism throughout the kibbutzim and marketplaces of the fledging Jewish state of Israel. The popularity of his writings among nonpracticing Jews and Gentiles served to spread his inclusionary message. According to Rabbi Kook, the Jewish nation corresponded to the heart of Adam Kadmon; but even this distinction had to be obliterated in the experience of Nothingness. His successors had to walk a fine line. For many, practicing Kabbalah meant choosing between traditional Orthodox Judaism and a form of universalism that bordered on heresy. It is important to note, however, that while the teachers in Kook's lineage accepted secular disciples, they themselves remained observant Jews. And this includes even the most liberal Kabbalists of the 1960s—those who welcomed women students, joined ecumenical movements, and incorporated popular Eastern meditation techniques into their teachings. Granted, today's feminist teachers have taken the secularization process a step further, but even they continue to base their interpretations of liturgy and ritual on the Torah.

So, does one have to be observant, or even Jewish, to practice Kabbalah? If one bases one's commitment solely on meditation, the answer is no. But given the fact that the language of kabbalistic meditation is Hebrew, and that its metaphors and symbols come from the Hebrew Bible, aspirants must possess at least some affinity for the Jewish tradition. Similarly, anyone can practice Christian contemplation or *zazen* or yoga meditation, but these can't be performed without using techniques and images that are steeped in Christian or Buddhist or Hindu traditions. In recent years, much has been said about mixing and matching various forms of spirituality, custom-tailoring a practice for the modern individual. Today you will find people calling themselves Ju-Bus (Jewish Buddhists), Jewish-Christians, Jewish-Hindus, Jewish-Sufis (Muslims), and Jewish-Wiccans (Goddess Worshipers). But I think they are talking less about their Jewish religious identity than about their Jewish ethnicity. The word after the hyphen refers to their spiritual practice. Such people do not consider themselves Kabbalists or Jewish mystics.

As we head toward the millennium, renewed interest in the Western monotheistic religions is likely to increase. Fundamentalisms and apocalyptic cults abound at such times; they are products of the spiritual hunger that characterizes endings and new beginnings. As this spiritual hunger grows, mysticism and secularism will undoubtedly bend to accommodate each other. Shifting cultural norms are sure to bring about changes in Jewish mysticism—perhaps even radical ones, such as the secularization of its constituency. But whatever happens, Torah-based meditation will continue to be the mainstay of the Kabbalah.

New Directions

In a world ruled by megabytes and sound bites, people are unlikely to spend their time trying to decipher ancient texts. A computer-educated generation will probably never get to know what it is to pore over a printed book, not to speak of a venerable handwritten manuscript. Adept at handling computer graphics programs, a new generation of Kabbalists might be encouraged to create their own mandalas for visualization. Such personal renderings of Ezekiel's

Chariot or the dancing letters of the sacred Names, for example, should not only enhance individual creativity, but should serve to fully engage practitioners and keep meditation from becoming stale. As a result, depending less on outmoded social customs, Kabbalists should take more responsibility for their practice than they did in the past. New bonds will form; mystical companionship will see greater equality, and a democratic distribution of roles will replace rigid, hierarchical forms. Twenty-first-century Kabbalah should see a dramatic change in the teacher-student relationship. Teachers will remain spiritual guides, but they will probably no longer be regarded as "experts" in every area of life. New emotional boundaries dividing meditative guidance from therapeutic, financial, and career advice should diminish the possibilities for exploitation and abuse on the part of both teachers and students. In the greater egalitarian setting that will mark the next century, mystical companions will no longer use titles such as "Master," "Rebbe," or "Tzaddik," but will refer to each other by their first names. Women teachers will more likely be giving instruction to students in distant parts of the world while seated in front of a computer than lecturing from behind a traditional *mechitzah*—the screen that hid the Baal Shem Tov's daughter from the gaze of her male disciples.

Continuing the Hasidic tradition, Kabbalists at all levels of spiritual development will serve in occupations other than clergy. But the times are past for Hasidim like my grandfather, who abandoned job and family for a leisurely thirteen-year stint at his rebbe's table. Globalization should increase the farflung nature of work, and, no less than other people, mystics will find themselves changing careers in the course of their working lives. But this will mean more time spent in raising the sparks from one's daily activities, and less in prayerful isolation. Faster and easier means of travel will allow Kabbalists to meet and meditate together more frequently, but for shorter periods.

Family and Community

Along with the radical changes wrought by technology in the world of work and communication, spiritual seekers in the twenty-first century will also have to adjust to new family and community configurations. The liberalizing trend begun by Rabbi Kook at the beginning of the century will become the norm, and the Kabbalah will grow more inclusive. It will not only embrace women, non-Orthodox Jews, and Gentiles, but unmarried couples, single parents, gays and lesbians, and others who do not conform to traditional standards of orthodoxy. Like all other spiritual disciplines, the Kabbalah will have to concede to the demands of a more secular world in order to accommodate its new constituency. Universalism and multiculturalism will characterize the twenty-first-century spiritual community in general. Though continuing to adhere to a uniquely Jewish form of meditation practice, Kabbalists will be less likely than their forebears to isolate themselves from the secular world. Even the model of the present-day Hasidic community will prove too sectarian for those seeking to close the gap between spiritual and everyday life.

Twenty-first-century spiritual people will be less likely to gather around a charismatic or prophetic figure, and living as "righteousness" will become the personal responsibility of every individual practitioner. Instead of conforming to ethical codes imposed on them as moral or religious duties, Kabbalists will themselves function as living expressions of the divine qualities inherent in the sefirot, and as sacred vessels for the powerful sparks hidden in the letters of their prayers. Ancient rituals will be charged with new life, as old cultural norms are expanded to embrace new ones. The practice of hitbodedut will be open to anyone who aspires to become one with No-thing. The ensuing infusion of kabbalistic symbolism into wedding ceremonies, funerals, bar and bat mitzvahs, and the celebration of the Sabbath will serve to enrich the lives of those seeking "relevancy" in the ancient traditions.

Widespread interest in Kabbalah will create new forms of dispensing a Hebrew education. Emphasis will be placed less on Torah study than on Torah practice. Rote teaching exercises will give way to the early incorporation of meditative awareness into Hebrew alphabet lessons and daily prayer. Children will be encouraged to explore the living meaning of the letters through drawing and visualization instead of memorization. Music and dance will introduce them to a sensory experience of the Torah, and divine immanence will be expressed by androgynous symbols.

No-thingness in a World of Things

I have just presented a highly optimistic scenario for twenty-first-century Jewish mysticism. Now let me pose a few hard questions.

1. *Amid the increasing technological din, won't it be harder to lose oneself in No-thingness?*

Yes, I'm sure it will. We have already seen how difficult it is to cultivate righteousness in a century characterized by violence, economic disparity, overstimulation by the media, and the commercialization of the sacred. I think it will be even more difficult to raise the sparks in a world of virtual reality.

2. *Will people be too numbed by suffering to care whether it is simulated or actually happening?*

Those who commit themselves to daily hitbodedut will not.

3. *Won't spiritual seekers be too mesmerized by the latest gadget to make time for meditation?*

They won't, once they see that its long-term benefits far outweigh the short-term stimulus provided by the gadgets.

4. *How will Kabbalists simplify their needs when the hardware ruling their lives grows more complex?*

By conducting their daily activities with a meditative attitude, and consciously using techniques based on the psychological insights of great forebears such as Rabbi Akiva, the Ari, and the Baal Shem Tov, Kabbalists will quite naturally simplify their needs. Without turning to asceticism or rejecting their circumstances, they will find that the encouragement of like-minded teachers and friends lightens the effort.

5. *In this context, what, specifically, can be done to avoid the powerful distractions and replenish the experience of No-thingness?*

Use the things of the world to recognize No-thing. By this I mean, approach everyday life as an ongoing opportunity for raising the sparks. Take a micro-moment for establishing a meditative attitude, whether that moment be painful or joyous or neutral. Practice hitbodedut everywhere, at all times. When tempted away from righteousness by idleness, anger, or greed, let yourself listen to the sounds of that moment until you are all ear, nothing but listening. Wrap yourself in listening until even the still, small voice of the moment has vanished and there is No-thing there at all.

Suggestions for Further Reading

Ariel, David. *The Mystic Quest*. New York: Schocken Books, 1988.

Armstrong, Karen. *A History of God*. New York: Knopf, 1993.

Bahya Ibn Pakuda. *The Book of Direction to the Duties of the Heart*. Translated by Menachem Mansoor. London: Routledge and Kegan Paul, 1973.

Besserman, Perle, ed. *The Way of the Jewish Mystics*. Boston: Shambhala Publications, 1994.

Bloom, Harold. *Kabbalah and Criticism*. New York: Seabury Press, 1975.

Buber, Martin. *Tales of the Hasidim: Early Masters*. New York: Schocken Books, 1975.

———. *Tales of the Hasidim: Later Masters*. New York: Schocken Books, 1948.

Cordovero, Moses. *The Palm Tree of Deborah*. Translated by Louis Jacobs. New York: Hermon Press, 1974.

Dan, Joseph, and Ronald C. Kiener. *The Early Kabbalah*. Mahwah, N.J.: Paulist Press, 1986.

Dan, Joseph. *Gershom Scholem and the Mystical Dimension of Jewish History*. New York: New York University Press, 1988.

Dov Baer of Lubavitch. *Tract on Ecstasy*. Translated by Louis Jacobs. London: Vallentine Mitchell, 1963.

Epstein, Perle [Besserman]. *Kabbalah: The Way of the Jewish Mystic*. Boston: Shambhala Publications, 1988.

Fine, Lawrence. *Safed Spirituality: Rules of Mystical Piety, The Beginning of Wisdom*. Mahwah, N.J.: Paulist Press, 1984.

Fisdel, Steven A. *The Practice of Kabbalah: Meditation in Judaism*. Northvale, N.J.: Jason Aronson, 1991.

Franck, Adolphe. *The Kabbalah*. New York: University Books, 1967.

Glotzer, Leonard R. *The Fundamentals of Jewish Mysticism*. Northvale, N.J.: Jason Aronson, 1992.

Gottlieb, Lynn. *She Who Dwells Within: A Feminist Vision of a Renewed Judaism*. San Francisco: Harper San Francisco, 1995.

Gutwirth, Israel. *The Kabbalah and Jewish Mysticism*. New York: Philosophical Library, 1987.

Harrelson, Walter. *From Fertility Cult to Worship*. New York: Doubleday, 1964.

Hoffman, Edward. *The Way of Splendor: Jewish Mysticism and Modern Psychology*. Boulder, Colo.: Shambhala Publications, 1981.

Idel, Moshe. *Kabbalah: New Perspectives*. New Haven: Yale University Press, 1988.

Kaplan, Aryeh. *The Aryeh Kaplan Reader*. Brooklyn: Mesorah Publications, 1990.

———. *The Bahir*. York Beach, Maine: Samuel Weiser, 1989.

———. *Inner Space*. Brooklyn: Maznaim Publishing Corp., 1990.

———. *Jewish Meditation*. New York: Schocken Books, 1985.

———. *The Light Beyond: Adventures in Hassidic Thought*. Brooklyn: Maznaim Publishing Corp., 1981.

———. *Meditation and Kabbalah*. York Beach, Maine: Samuel Weiser, 1986.

———. *Meditation and the Bible*. York Beach, Maine: Samuel Weiser, 1978.

———. *Sefer Yetzirah: The Book of Creation*. York Beach, Maine: Samuel Weiser, 1990.

Labowitz, Shoni. *Miraculous Living: A Guided Journey through the Ten Gates of the Tree of Life*. New York: Simon and Schuster, 1997.

Luzzatto, Moses. *General Principles of the Kabbalah*. New York: Samuel Weiser, 1970.

Luzzatto, Moshe Chayim. *The Way of God*. Translated by Aryeh Kaplan. New York: Philip Feldheim Publishers, 1983.

Matt, Daniel. *The Essential Kabbalah: The Heart of Jewish Mysticism*. San Francisco: Harper San Francisco, 1995.

Matt, Daniel (trans.). *Zohar: The Book of Enlightenment*. Mahwah, N.J.: Paulist Press, 1983.

Meltzer, David. *The Anatomy of God*. New York: Ktav Publishing House, 1973.

———. *The Secret Garden*. New York: Seabury Press, 1976.

Munk, Rabbi Michael L. *The Wisdom in the Hebrew Alphabet.* New York: Mesorah Publications, 1983.

Patai, Raphael. *The Jewish Alchemists.* Princeton: Princeton University Press, 1994.

Ponce, Charles. *Kabbalah.* Wheaton, Ill.: Quest Books, 1980.

Schaya, Leo. *The Universal Meaning of the Kabbalah.* Translated by Nancy Pearson. London: George Allen and Unwin, 1971.

Scholem, Gershom. *Kabbalah.* New York: Meridian, 1978.

————. *Major Trends in Jewish Mysticism.* New York: Schocken Books, 1974.

————. *On the Kabbalah and Its Symbolism.* New York: Schocken Books, 1978.

————. *On the Mystical Shape of the Godhead.* New York: Schocken Books, 1991.

————. *Zohar: The Book of Splendor.* New York: Schocken Books, 1973.

Shapiro, Rabbi Rami. *Minyan: The Tenfold Path of Jewish Spiritual Practice.* New York: Bell Tower, 1997.

Sperling, Harry, and Maurice Simon, trans. *The Zohar.* 5 vols. London: Soncino Press, 1984.

Steinsaltz, Adin. *The Thirteen-Petalled Rose.* New York: Basic Books, 1980.

Tishby, Isaiah, ed. *The Wisdom of the Zohar.* 3 vols. New York: Oxford University Press, 1989.

Trachtenberg, Joshua. *Jewish Magic and Superstition.* New York: Atheneum, 1977.

Zalman, Rabbi Schneur. *Likutei Amarim: Tanya.* London: Kehot Publication Society, 1973.

Videotape

Gitlin, Harvey, and Edward Hoffman. *A Mystical Journey through the Hebrew Alphabet.* VoVids, 1989.

Index